ROWENA MABBOTT

Travel Light With Kids

How to Travel as a Family with Carry-On Luggage Only

RoMa Press

A catalogue record for this book is available from the National Library of Australia.

First edition

ISBN: 978-0-6486030-8-5

This book was professionally typeset on Reedsy.
Find out more at reedsy.com

For my family: James, Oscar, and Nicholas, who were willing to try travelling with only carry-on luggage when I first suggested it more than a decade ago.

Thank you for coming along for the ride.

"He who would travel happily must travel light."

– Antoine de Saint-Exupéry

Contents

IV Pulling it all together

Foreword

You are a complete and total person.
Your anxieties, fears and other hang-ups are simply part of who
you are.
Do you want to carry them with you when you travel?
Or are you travelling to escape the everyday and to become a
better version of yourself?

While this book is specifically written for those who wish to travel with less, that is, with only carry-on luggage on aeroplanes, the guidelines and suggestions contained within apply to all types of transportation.

However, if your family trip or trips involve only driving, with no other transportation, you have fewer restrictions. Therefore, while these tips are still helpful, they may not be as applicable.

Therefore, please read the book with the understanding that these are suggestions and tips designed to help you pack less when travelling by plane or train, where oversized luggage would be a considerable inconvenience, hassle, and possible hindrance to the enjoyment of your family trip.

How to use this book

This book presents content in a simple, easy-to-understand, and easy-to-implement way. It's a short book, and can be read in one afternoon.

For ease, throughout I refer to travelling with carry-on luggage only as 'travelling light'.

There are four (4) sections within the book.

Part One covers WHY:

The first part explains why we travel light and the benefits of travelling light, and includes questions to help determine whether this type of travel is right for you and your family.

Part Two explores MINDSET:

Specifically, we examine the mindset shifts required to adopt a more minimalist approach, as well as common myths and misconceptions. In this section, we also discuss planning and share some hard-earned (by us) tips for what works well when travelling with less. Additionally, we share sustainability tips in this section.

Part Three covers PRACTICALITIES:

This section provides factors and tips to consider when selecting bags, clothing, and toiletries, along with specific guidance on packing your items into a compact bag. This part also includes information about the items we often think we need when travelling with children, such as extra changes of clothes, toys, and entertainment.

Part Four captures FINAL WORDS:

Here you'll find the TL;DR (Too Long Didn't Read) summary and the appendix, which includes a few of our packing lists with the exact items we packed for travelling to various locations. These examples show what items can fit in a small carry-on bag, rather than serving as a checklist.

You may be tempted to skip directly to **Part 3,** jumping straight to the practicalities, hoping to find numerous 'packing hacks' and similar advice. However, I recommend that you refrain from doing that.

Instead, read the book in order. Each chapter builds on the earlier one, and takes you on a journey to shift you from apprehension about whether travelling in this way is possible, to slowly building your knowledge and confidence that it is indeed possible, if you make a few adjustments to how you've thought about packing until now.

Are you ready to change the way you pack?

Let's get started.

Introduction

"The extra luggage of indiscriminate dreams, desires and
attachments will make your life's journey miserable."
– *Mata Amritanandamayi*

Cast your mind back sixty or seventy years, when people generally had less stuff. Think about the images of children being sent to far-flung places during the World War II evacuations. They arrived with nothing more than the clothes on their backs and a tiny handheld suitcase that may contain a change of underpants and, perhaps, if they were fortunate, their Sunday best outfit.

While we fantasise about grand, high-sea travels with big container chests full of possessions, multiple dinner dresses, and outfit changes, that is not how most people lived. Travel was so exorbitantly expensive that it was predominantly reserved for the very wealthy.

I suspect this is why we frequently misrepresent how people travelled in the past.

The common folk like you and I would have had few possessions. Therefore, they would have travelled with a simple bag containing a change of clothes and maybe one nicer outfit just in case they were invited somewhere or had planned to visit a location that required more smart attire.

Whether we realise it or not, for the vast majority of us, this is part of our collective consciousness regarding travel. It is a deeply held belief that we need to change our outfits for every possible occasion we may encounter. Popular culture, including cinema, books, and magazine articles, has long encouraged and fostered this view.

And it's not just when we travel. The belief that we need to have a specific look for certain occasions drives most of our purchasing decisions.

And this comes into play even when we are looking to travel light.

How many of us have purchased something specifically for a trip? A new pair of trousers marketed explicitly as ideal for travel? A different or new backpack, handbag, or security item?

There are entire businesses whose focus is on providing you with items specifically for travelling, and others that focus on providing new items for travelling light.

The struggle we face when travelling with carry-on luggage only is symptomatic of where we have evolved as a society. As we increasingly attribute self-worth and value to possessions, we struggle to pare down and determine which are truly valuable and necessary to take with us when we travel.

Also, our inability to select a handful of items to travel with is indicative of the hidden anxieties many people struggle with in their lives. Our possessions help us feel secure, or at least that is what we believe.

Based on what people have shared with me, this is the crux of why many people struggle to travel light. It always comes down to fear: What if I need this thing? What if the weather changes? What if I can't get that medicine? What if I don't feel like wearing that particular item?

Has a myriad of choices become so customary that it's stopping us from travelling with less? This is a genuine question for both when we physically travel to another location and throughout our lives in general.

Our possessions are a big part of our sense of self and identity (particularly clothes!). Our clothes, then, are an area where people often confuse themselves about how to travel light. Clothes feel like armour in situations where we feel uncomfortable or uncertain, and so having just the 'right' clothes for each and every circumstance can feel like protection. Certainly, in some circumstances, having the correct attire is very important. Particularly if you are pursuing a specific sport, attending religious events or venues, or need particular clothing to protect your body from the elements.

But we all know what clothes make us feel best. And I would hazard a guess that you already have them in your wardrobe. You already wear them most of the time. You don't need new ones; you need to find the ones that make you feel fantastic right now. Most of us are familiar with our personal clothing preferences. We already own them. THESE are your travel clothes.

Which is where this book is different.

You already have everything you need to travel light. There is no need to purchase anything (except for this book) as you already have everything you love, which is the only thing we want you to take with you.

Which is as valid for travelling as it is for living your everyday life.

Before we dive in, an important note. While this book focuses on how to travel light (carry-on luggage only) with kids, the ideas, insights, and tips shared are equally valid for those travelling without children.

I

Why should you travel light?

"Adopt a traveller's mentality. When we travel, we take only what we need for the journey. As a result, we feel lighter, freer, more flexible. Adopting a traveller's mindset for life provides the same benefit—not just for a weeklong vacation, but in everything we do. Adopt a mindset that seeks to carry only what you need for the journey."

— *Joshua Becker*

1

Why We Travel Light

"Travel opens your heart, broadens your mind and fills your life
with stories to tell."
— *Paula Bendfeldt*

We were not light travellers before becoming parents; even the first few trips as new parents were far from it. It took us until our eldest child was seven and our youngest was four years old before we felt ready to attempt travelling with both smaller and fewer bags.

Unfortunately, before this 'awakening', our travel history is filled with many rather embarrassing stories of having far too much luggage.

As an eighteen-year-old, travelling to the UK to live and work for a year, I had an enormous suitcase (weighing over 35 kilograms!), a stuffed backpack, and a 10-kilogram carry-on bag. I then had to juggle and struggle with these three hefty and cumbersome items by myself across the cobblestones in freezing-cold Oxford as the January winds whipped around me, and tears of frustration crept down my face. It was neither safe nor graceful for a single female to travel with such a ridiculous amount of luggage. It was incredibly hard work.

A few years later, I was backpacking through Africa and Europe, and although I had shifted to a single backpack (with a zip-off day pack), it was still an enormous eighty-litre bag, carried on my then fifty-three-kilogram (116-pound) frame. An indication of how much I brought that was unnecessary includes carrying a one-kilogram book in my backpack for six weeks, envisaging that I would read it on long-haul flights. Of course, I never cracked the book's spine or read a single page. Instead, I carried the equivalent of an extra one-kilogram brick around in my backpack, apparently just for the fun of it!

Fast forward a few years again, and we were on our honeymoon. We arrived at the car hire place at Heathrow Airport in London, looking forward to a few days in the English countryside, only to discover that they had upgraded us to a Mazda MX-5. (For those without car-mad children, a Mazda MX-5 is a small convertible sports car.) We were delighted but also mortified. There was no way we could accept it, as our luggage (for just the two of us) was more than would fit in the MX5's boot. Even though the boot could accommodate a complete set of golf clubs, we couldn't squeeze our three giant bags into it. It was not a great start to travelling light as a couple.

A few years later, we were travelling for Christmas. We were about to take our first overseas trip with our firstborn son. He was 13 months old, and we were heading from the Australian summer to the UK to spend Christmas with family and hopefully, with snow. Our bags were packed, along with a child's car seat, a stroller, a booster seat for the dining table, and various other essentials that we anticipated we'd need. Of course, we overpacked, ridiculously so.

The worst part was that the airline lost our luggage on both the way there and the return journey. On the way over, they lost the stroller and the car seat. On the way back, ALL our bags went missing for five days. As most people can confirm, the experience of lost luggage, missing for multiple days, is not enjoyable. It's more stressful and makes it much worse when travelling with a small child.

Years passed with many domestic trips within Australia. Some were only a short, one-hour flight; others required two flights, meaning five to six hours in the air. Gradually, we were learning to carry less. After several domestic trips where we were travelling lighter and lighter, our first big overseas trip with the children approached.

We booked the flights six months in advance and began pre-booking accommodation. It was time for me to research.

The idea of travelling with a lot less came, innocently enough, when I Googled 'capsule wardrobe'. I was looking for suggestions on how to manage the same clothes for three weeks. Hours turned to days, which turned to weeks, and almost months of research into clothing choices, bag choices, and ultimately, how to travel carry-on only.

Once the idea took hold, it was hard to shake. Travelling with only carry-on-sized luggage became a goal, which meant packing light became a mission.

After I'd decided we would completely change our travel tradition and pack light rather than overpack, the research began in earnest.

I started searching the web for any information I could find about travelling with only carry-on luggage with children. More hours would pass, and I would read hundreds of articles, blog posts, and suggested packing lists. Not even one included anything useful about travelling light with children. Indeed, there were plenty of valuable references, from capsule wardrobes to zip-off trousers (shudder) and the best type of backpack to use or not use.

But nothing told me *how* to make travelling light with kids a reality for my family and me.

Which is partly why I decided to write this guide. From the hours I spent researching and our experience travelling light with our kids to multiple destinations at different times of the year and across various age groups, we knew we had enough experience to share our knowledge with you.

With good planning and a wealth of research behind us, we embarked on our first family trip overseas in December 2014, with only carry-on luggage.

And we haven't looked back! For more than a decade, we have travelled with carry-on luggage only on all flights—both international and domestic.

If you're reading this and thinking, 'I'm not sure I could do that', in the next chapter, I share some of the benefits we've experienced, which I hope will help you start to see how truly transformative travelling with less can be.

2

Benefits of Travelling Light as a Family

"Limits give you clarity, focus, and purpose. They also give you a feeling of safety, and safety gives you the confidence to explore."
Annie Auerbach

This chapter aims to help you see the significant benefits of travelling light. Below are the main advantages we see. But there will be others! Everyone's experience is different, and here I've captured the main benefits we continue to experience. Travelling (and living) with less is not only a way to save money and reduce our environmental footprint, it can also inspire us to move more freely, think more creatively and be open to new experiences.

Why is this important?

When you first consider packing light, carrying only a carry-on bag, or using smaller luggage, it may feel quite challenging. However, keeping the benefits in mind will help you stay focused and see it through to the end. And when you do, you'll feel a sense of accomplishment in mastering the art of efficient packing.

Our focus on carry-on-only travel stemmed from our desire to avoid lost luggage on our first family trip to the USA. We knew that with the winter weather, the number of flights we had and short stays in multiple locations, lost luggage would be a significant headache and not something we had time to deal with.

We initially chose to travel light to avoid something. Still, after that trip, we realised the benefits, and these positive outcomes kept us focused on going smaller and smaller, which we have done.

Please keep in mind that all of these benefits apply to individual, couple, and family travel, and are even more appreciated when travelling with children.

Time saved

When you travel light, with carry-on luggage only, there is no need to queue at the airport to check your bags. Avoiding those huge queues of people can save you and your family many, many hours of standing around and slowly shuffling towards the check-in desk.

Walking straight to the gate after passing through security and passport control ensures a seamless, stress-free start to your adventure.

No waiting

Similarly, when you arrive at your destination, travelling carry-on only means there is no waiting there either.

Not for you, still waiting at the luggage carousel as the minutes pass by, and before you know it, it's been 45 minutes waiting for your luggage. No, you are on your way! Easily walk off your chosen transport (plane, train, bus or ferry) and onto your next destination. Whether that be a shuttle bus, local transport, or something else, you're already exploring your new location while everyone else is still waiting for their luggage.

Ease

Ease is one of the advantages of travelling with less. Ease of dressing, ease of movement and ease of decision-making.

Let's address each of these briefly.

Ease of dressing:

Of course, with a smaller bag, you can only fit so much in. And so, selecting what to wear each day becomes easier because there are fewer choices. Interestingly, we didn't find this restrictive at all. We gained a sense of calm confidence, as the morning angst and drama about clothing choices were no longer an issue.

Ease of movement:

With only one small bag per person, manoeuvring through airports, train stations, and on and off public transport is easy. And it's far easier to navigate crowded places. You can have your hands free for other things, which is definitely an added benefit, especially when travelling with young children.

Stairs are not a problem when your luggage is small. It's easier to move with elegance, grace and dexterity when you are not struggling to wheel an oversized bag or heft a huge duffel or backpack. Additionally, you won't experience back, neck or shoulder pain, allowing you to continue moving and enjoying your holiday.

Ease of decision-making:

Again, with a small, carry-on-size bag, (most) decisions are easier. Indeed, decisions about what to pack are simplified — it becomes a matter of whether you really need it and whether it will fit.

But other decisions, too, are made more easily when you travel light.

- You experience less decision fatigue when selecting your daily wear.
- Decisions about whether to walk to your accommodation or to catch a taxi.
- Decisions about whether you need to pre-book a special transfer to accommodate your family and all your luggage, or whether the local train will suffice.
- Decisions about leaving your luggage at a left luggage depot whilst you explore the city.

All these decisions become easier or irrelevant when you travel light with only small carry-on luggage.

Freedom

When you pack light, there's no need to babysit your bags; they're compact and with you, especially if they're carry-on or smaller. This liberates you to hop on and off planes, buses, trains, ferries, and more without worrying about your luggage.

Flexibility

Flexibility is a major benefit of travelling light. It certainly is one of our favourite reasons!

When you travel light with small, easy-to-carry bags, you increase your flexibility. Your luggage is with you while you wait for flights; it is not checked and remains accessible. Therefore, when an option arises to shift to an earlier flight, you are well-placed to take that opportunity!

Or, perhaps less excitingly, but still a win, when two elevators are out of order, and there is only one operating, with a massive queue of people waiting for it, travelling light means you are more flexible. You can carry your luggage up the stairs with minimal inconvenience and be on your way.

Travelling light gives you flexibility. Being flexible enhances your travel experience.

Cost-saving

You knew this one would make it to the top ten, right? However, interestingly, this was—and still is not—one of the main reasons we choose to travel carry-on luggage only.

We include it here because travelling light, particularly with carry-on-only luggage, can potentially save money.

We won't list all the cost savings you can make (it's not that type of book), but here are a few where we know travelling light makes a big difference.

Cheaper airfares

Increasingly, on certain airlines, especially in Europe and North America, airfares are seat-only, and checked luggage is an added cost. By travelling carry-on only, you and your family can avoid these additional charges and take advantage of the many super-discounted airfares that include carry-on luggage as standard, whereas adding checked luggage often costs significantly more.

Cheaper transportation costs

When you can easily manage your luggage, and your children can too, walking becomes a viable option, which can significantly reduce additional expenses associated with other forms of travel. This not only eliminates the costs of fuel or public transit fares but also allows you to enjoy the fresh air and the sights of your surroundings, familiarising yourself with local landmarks. By choosing to walk, you can not only save money but also build environmentally friendly habits and expand and enrich your travel experience.

Avoid additional charges

Similar to airlines, we have found that certain USA and European railways charge additional luggage fees for 'excess' luggage. Whilst most of us assume 'excess' luggage is above twenty or thirty kilograms (the figures the airlines use), on some railways, 'excess' is anything above ten kilograms, which means that even some airline-approved carry-on-size bags would be classified as overweight. You can save on the fees and the hassle by travelling as lightly as possible.

Limited space

Okay, so this doesn't sound like a significant cost-saving. But it can be! We have found that knowing we have limited space in our bags can help us avoid spending money on souvenirs and other items. By considering whether we love the item AND have space to carry it, we often don't end up buying whatever item we were lusting after at that moment. Thus, a solid way to save money is simply not to spend it. But it's also a way to save time and effort in maintaining or using that item in the future.

A side note – not once have we regretted something we didn't buy!

Simplicity

The packing-up process is streamlined when you have fewer items, allowing you to get going faster. You also need less time to tidy up and pack when checking out and leaving your accommodation, which is a major benefit when the early-rising young children have become sleeping-in teens! It's also streamlined and straightforward when you get home, since everyone has much less to unpack.

Preparedness

You will have given your packing selections more thought, so you will be more prepared when you arrive, simply because you've already considered the activities, the weather, and other factors. You will feel prepared when you arrive, which will help build your confidence.

Confidence

Being well-prepared instils confidence in both adults and children, especially when you are travelling light with fewer items. This confidence grows as you realise that you have everything you actually need (the essentials) without the burden of excess baggage.

Independence and responsibility

Of course, another major bonus of travelling light is that your children learn independence and responsibility. To travel with carry-on-only bags, each family member must have their own bag, which they can wheel or carry themselves.

The sense of confidence, capability, and independence that comes with being responsible for one's own belongings cannot be underestimated. As parents, we all want our children to exhibit independence, whether it be the ability to think for themselves, make their own decisions, or possess an independent spirit. These are qualities we wish to foster in our kids.

When children have their own bag containing their belongings, and must be responsible for them, they are learning a valuable life skill and lesson. We are each responsible for ourselves in this life. As adults, we are expected to manage our belongings. Allowing our children to practice this skill in advance is beneficial.

Encouraging your child to be independent and responsible, with all their belongings packed in their own bag, is a clear benefit of travelling light.

Holiday feeling

Related to Ease (*see above*), travelling light maximises the feeling of being on holiday.

Travelling light with kids can feel easier than your everyday life. The holiday vibe is magnified when packing up to move on to your next destination is a breeze. With fewer items to maintain and therefore pack, packing up is simpler and easier, and departure is faster, which in turn means you enjoy your holiday more!

And even better, travelling light helps you retain that holiday feeling when you get home. Once home, with very little to unpack or wash, you won't spend hours or days washing. Instead, the holiday feeling of relaxation and happiness lasts much longer.

Indeed, we have found this to be a major benefit. When travelling with small children, getting up and making an early departure with minimal fuss (because we haven't got much stuff to pack) is advantageous. Many times, it meant taking an earlier train or getting on the road before peak-hour traffic was achievable.

Arriving home without needing to spend an entire day unpacking and washing is also a bonus for weary travellers, especially parents.

Joy

The joy you feel and provide when you travel light is a significant benefit.

A simple example is the delighted smile on your taxi or transfer bus driver's face when they see how little luggage you have, meaning it will fit easily into their already full boot.

We have experienced similar interactions with shuttle and minibus drivers, airline check-in personnel, and train conductors. Those delighted smiles have made us feel amazing and have always greatly boosted our well-being. Okay, honestly, it occasionally even made us feel a little smug.

Life lessons

What is it that we most want our children to learn in life? Are there life lessons we feel it's our job as parents to instil and impart?

By travelling light, we help our children feel confident and capable, making them happier in themselves. And isn't that why we travel: for the joy, excitement, adventure, and new experiences?

As parents, we can facilitate this for our children. We can instil in them the love of travel and the delight of visiting new cultures, meeting new people and experiencing new tastes. Add to this the responsibility for their belongings, and they feel empowered, as do we.

Less is more

We saved this one for last. In a world of contrasts in wealth and possessions, and in a consumeristic, materialistic culture, learning that having less stuff can mean more of other things is a huge benefit we have experienced from travelling light with our kids.

Children, like adults, enjoy accumulating belongings. But when we travel with fewer items, we realise that more stuff is not the answer. Having fewer things means we can say yes to more opportunities. Carrying fewer things means we have more flexibility, and we'd add, possibly, more fun too!

Since our first travelling light adventure, this benefit and lesson have had the most ongoing impact. This benefit, experienced for the first time in December 2014, changed the pattern of our family life, both when travelling and at home.

I hope reading these benefits has sparked some ideas for why travelling light might be a positive experience for you and your family. In the next chapter, I share how to determine whether travelling carry-on-only is achievable for you and your family.

3

Is Carry-On-Only Travel Right for You and Your Family?

"If you challenge yourself, you will grow."
Sir Richard Branson.

After reading about some of the benefits of travelling light in the previous chapter, I hope you are starting to feel excited about the opportunity to do the same.

However, the key question you might be asking yourself is probably: "Is this right for my family and me?"

Let's now discuss some important information about the types of people who are suitable for carry-on-only travel.

Carry on only travel suits people who:

- Want to save time and money when travelling.
- Want simplicity in their travel life and want to enjoy the travel, and not worry about packing and all their stuff.
- Enjoy lower stress and anxiety, and wish to use less brain space

worrying about their luggage, both during preparation time and especially on travel days.

- Enjoy getting a good night's sleep before they travel, as they are not worried about fitting everything in or 'what if' scenarios.
- Want time actually to travel and enjoy their experiences, and do not want to waste time waiting for or checking luggage.
- Are tired of searching for the next travel gadget or a new bag. Once you have the right gear for travelling, a carry-on bag is all you'll use again and again. For example, items we invested in for our 2014 trip are still in use more than a decade later.
- Are ready for a change and a little challenge.
- Are willing to try something different, even if it feels a little hard at first.
- Understand that this way of travelling may require new routines, different products, and a different outlook on what makes a great travel wardrobe.
- Have a physical need to pack lighter, just as we did when we had two small children. The key was to have access for holding hands with a small child, and not need to lug large bags. You can manage your own luggage without assistance when travelling with carry-on only or smaller bags. It is within your control, and you maintain your independence. This is terrific for people of all ages and stages.
- Are prepared to do the work. Yes, it will require extra work, more than tossing as many clothes as will fit into your large case.

Is that you? Can you say yes to most of this list?

If so, congratulations! You ARE the type of person who can travel with smaller, more manageable luggage and enjoy the many benefits that come with it.

Please note, generally, it's one or both parents who start thinking about travelling with less, not the children. If that's you (hello!), this list is essential, as you'll most likely be the one driving the change for your family.

There may be some initial hesitation, or, like us, you might find that once you explain and show* your family members how transformative travelling with less can be, they become lifelong converts, just as my family has.

*showing might involve physically laying out all the items that can be included in the small bag!

I hope you are feeling excited about the prospect of travelling with less! Next, I'll share the mindset shifts needed to transition from being an overpacker to packing only what you need.

II

Mindset and Planning

Change the way you think to change the way you travel.

4

Mindset Shifts

"The difficulty lies not so much in developing new ideas as in escaping from old ones."
– John Maynard Keynes

Congratulations — you've determined that you might be the type of person who can travel with less!

Now, here's the big breakthrough takeaway that will make this happen for you:

Mindset is key to travelling light, not packing hacks.

Packing hacks are often just gimmicks designed to get you to buy things you don't need. Instead, adopting a *packing light mindset* will help you pack less and better.

Doing the inner work, that is, changing your mindset about how you pack for travelling, is vital for successful packing and travelling light.

Of course, you can jump right into throwing clothes in a bag, but that will not guarantee you success. More likely, you will default to your usual practice and end up overpacking.

Instead, take some time to grasp the mindset shifts required to travel successfully with fewer clothing items and fewer items overall, resulting in lighter, carry-on-only luggage.

Here are a few mindset shifts to help you embrace travelling light and have your family travel with only carry-on luggage or less.

You will need to re-wear items

You will need to accept that you'll be wearing items more than once. Yes, this will mean you'll appear in the same top or jacket in photos. But who cares? We travel for the experience in the moment, not the images. Photos are simply for prompting our memory. Now, I suspect you've jumped forward and realised if you're rewearing clothes, that will entail washing. Before you baulk at the prospect of doing hours of laundry, know that many clothes, especially middle or outer layers and heavier items like jeans, can be aired rather than washed, and they will be fine for a second, third, fourth or even fifth day. Hang them on a hanger overnight with the wardrobe door open, or take them into the shower room and the steam can help refresh them.

Laundry *(see tip #7 in Chapter 7)* is possible even in a hotel sink, making it an easy way to wash underwear and socks daily or at least regularly.

Embrace a travel uniform

You must adjust to having a travel uniform, especially for long or big travel days. For instance, we typically wear our heaviest clothing, like jeans and boots, on travel days. We then establish two to three 'uniforms' from the clothes and outfits that have already been selected and planned. Yes, we often each wear similar clothing in our photos, which streamlines the number of items we need to pack. And we've never looked back at our pictures and felt disappointed that we were in the same jacket/sweater/scarf as two days earlier.

Simplicity and choice create more value

You learn to appreciate your items and use them in new or different ways than you might when you're at home. With limited choices, you will appreciate the value of a single item more.

This focus on simplicity means you will have time and energy to focus on what truly matters in the travel experience: the actual travel and experiences, not your clothes and luggage. Thus, the added value outweighs the 'cost' of having less.

EXAMPLE:

For our boys, we still pack long-sleeved cotton button-down shirts, which are versatile enough to be worn on their own, as a layer over a t-shirt, as a layer between a long-sleeved thermal and a woollen sweater, or as an extra mid-layer when four or more layers are worn to keep warm.

Travel is temporary

Remember, travel is temporary, and the limited choices are not forever! This restricted wardrobe and accessories are only for this particular trip, whether it's seven, fourteen, twenty-one days or more. Knowing that your limited wardrobe will only be in use for a short time makes it easier to accept and even embrace. Who knows, you might even enjoy it!

You need less than you think

Most of the things we pack are 'nice to have' rather than necessities. One key thing we have learnt after multiple trips travelling with less each time is that we need significantly less than we initially thought.

Not having something you 'could have packed' is not necessarily a failure or a bad thing. More often than not, you don't even miss it!

Pack for likely, not maybe

When we pack light, we do so with logic and reason, based on what is likely to happen – not just when there's a slight chance of something occurring, but also when something is more than likely to be needed.

EXAMPLE:

When we took a trip to Tasmania, I'd been watching the weather forecast and knew a cold snap was on the way. It would be cold and wet on the sixth day of our eight-day trip. Despite the added bulk in our small bags, we each packed packable rain jackets, which was very lucky, as the weather turned severe and the forecast rain turned into sleet, then snow. But because we had packed based on what was likely, as determined by our research, we were absolutely fine.

Make it happen. Your actions:

- Review the above mindset shifts.
- Think through the reality of each of these for your travel plans. Be realistic. Do they feel achievable? Or a step too far?
- Even if they feel daunting now, consider how you can embrace them to travel lighter than you currently do.

Mindset changes are key to packing light successfully. And, realistically, you need to adopt them all, or you'll likely struggle to pack small or carry-on only.

You may now be feeling a little rattled by the required mindset shifts, or, conversely, excited about the challenge. Next up, I'll discuss and dispel some myths and misconceptions about travelling light.

5

Myths and Misconceptions About Travelling Light

"You don't have to be rich to travel well."
– Eugene Fodor

In this chapter, I share some of the many excuses, myths, and misconceptions we have heard from friends, family, and other travellers about why they cannot travel light. And of course, I dispel many of these excuses and myths!

Myth 1: The only reason to travel light is to save money

Confirmed and Busted:

Yes, this is true. Travelling light *can* save money, which is undoubtedly a significant benefit for many people.

Travelling with less means you can often pay less for your airfare (*see Chapter 2*). Many airlines, both domestic and international, offer seat-only airfares. These include the option to bring a carry-on bag, but that is the only additional option. Often, you pay extra for food, entertainment, pillows, blankets and other services that can make a flight more comfortable. Therefore, if you are happy to fly without these services, you can save money by travelling light!

But saving money is not the only reason to travel light. There are many other reasons to travel light as well.

Our favourite reasons to travel light are the ease of movement and the freedom gained when you travel with less (*see Chapter 2*). Another is the simplified approach to life that comes from travelling with fewer belongings (*see Chapter 14*).

Travelling light certainly can save you money, but it's not the sole reason to travel this way. That said, if saving money is a major reason you want to travel light, we encourage you to go for it!

Myth 2: Travelling light is hard and next to impossible with kids, especially when they are small and need so much stuff.

Busted: Yes, travelling with really young children can be hard. And yes, travelling light with infants (still in nappies/diapers) can add complexity regardless of whether you are travelling light or with checked baggage. However, it's not impossible.

We've done it, and plenty of others manage it. It is doable.

The most important aspect of travelling with very young children is planning (*see Chapter 6*). By spending adequate time planning and researching options for renting specific items at your destination, or considering purchasing them only if needed, you can still travel light. Once you've done that, it is less complicated.

By buying this book, you are well on your way to getting started. Plus, the benefits of travelling with less stuff are totally worth it for you and your kids.

Myth 3: You must wear unfashionable 'travel' clothes to travel light

Busted: Ugh. No way. Let's be honest, some travel clothes are truly hideous. There is no way we would even attempt to travel light if it meant wearing ugly, multi-purpose clothing. We all like to look nice, whether in our hometown of Sydney, Australia or walking the Champs-der-Elysées in Paris. And certainly, none of us wants to have our clothes scream, 'Look at me! I'm a tourist!' It attracts the wrong type of attention.

With planning and consideration, it is perfectly possible to travel light and feel good wearing your regular clothes. That is, the clothes you already own, wear and love. This is also ideal for budget-conscious individuals who prefer to make minimal additional purchases. (*see Chapter 16 / Appendix for our packing lists, including specific clothes packed.*)

Myth 4: Travelling light means I don't have choices in my clothing or shoes (also expressed as 'I like options')

Busted: With good advance planning, you can carry multiple outfit changes, look and feel good, and have at least two pairs of shoes. We have even managed three pairs of shoes in luggage that weighed less than seven kilograms!

For true fashionistas (female and male) or those with foot issues, the thought of having only one or two pairs of shoes may be reason enough never to try travelling light. And that's okay — it's not for everyone.

But it comes down to a question of desire. No, not the desire to have more shoes! The desire to travel with ease, grace and flexibility. The desire to travel light. The desire to experience more from life and be a role model to our kids.

The key to feeling like you have plenty of choice and not getting sick of the one or two pairs of shoes you brought is to plan ahead and know your style. I know packing and travel planning can be tricky, so I've written an entire chapter about it (*see Chapter 6*).

Myth 5: My shoes and clothes are heavy, so I can't travel light

Busted: Oh, this is an old faithful excuse. My husband said this when I first suggested we try travelling light! And as my boys have grown into teenagers and young men, they have even trotted this one out a few times.

Indeed, many men's clothes, especially shoes, weigh more than those of children or women. And as children grow into teenagers and young adults, this applies even more so. Nevertheless, this is not a sufficient

35

excuse.

It simply means you need to get creative and consider what you actually *need* to bring versus what you'd like to bring. Streamlining to only necessities helps, as does selecting clothing that meets the needs of your travel environments. Small swaps can make all the difference. For example, a light-weight cotton or linen long-sleeved button-down shirt can weigh less than a heavy cotton t-shirt. It looks smarter, can be worn on more occasions and in different temperatures, acts as a layering piece, and provides increased sun protection. In our view, that's a win!

Myth 6: I can't travel light, as I might get stuck in an emergency (also expressed as 'I need to pack a lot of stuff 'just in case' I might need it')

Busted: True confession—I used to travel with this mindset, and I still find it can pop up when packing. It's one of the most used excuses I hear. Let's bust this one open.

Most of the items that are squeezed in 'just in case' are never used. They are packed to provide a sense of safety and security and perhaps bring a little comfort of home. But they add weight and take up valuable space in your bag, which is already limited. On rare occasions when you need something you don't have, there is a good chance you can source it locally. There are some exceptions: if you travel through developing or third-world countries, or to incredibly remote locations, or have a specific medical or health need.

However, for most of us, when we are travelling with our children, that's unlikely to be the case. Substitution, doing without, making do, or purchasing locally can solve 99% of the issues you pack for 'just in case.'

(For a list of the items we reject as 'Just In Case' packing, see Chapter 11.)

Make it happen. Your actions:

- Review the above myths and misconceptions.
- Be honest about how many of these you have (previously) said/believed/used as an excuse.
- Assess the myths and misconceptions you've previously believed, and think through how you'll address these now that you are changing the way you view packing for travel. For example, you'll no longer pack 'just in case' items.

I hope that reviewing these myths and misconceptions has prompted you to rethink some of the reasons you've given yourself for why travelling light is too difficult. Next, I'll share and explain more about why planning is essential for successfully travelling with less.

6

Planning: Before You Travel

"If you fail to plan, you are planning to fail."
— *Benjamin Franklin*

Depending on how long you're travelling for and the destinations or countries you're visiting (and their customs and culture), as well as the activities you intend to do there, it may feel very challenging to travel with only seven kilograms of luggage per person.

Therefore, we encourage you to take the time to research, consider, and plan. Effective planning can make the difference between a fantastic trip where your luggage is simply that, and one where it becomes an integral part of your experience. And that is not necessarily a good outcome— lost luggage, we are looking at you!

On some trips, larger luggage is necessary to ensure you are adequately equipped for the desired experiences, such as a ski or diving trip. Indeed, taking the family skiing overseas may require more equipment and clothing than can reasonably fit in a small carry-on bag. But even then, hiring skis and clothes at your destination is an option to consider as part of your planning.

Let's get into it.

Pre-packing planning

Anticipation is often half the fun. Studies have shown that we are often happier during the eight weeks *leading up to the holiday* than during the holiday itself. Amazing, right? So, enjoying a great holiday or vacation before you've even left is possible. How does that work?

Well, it's all about anticipation and planning.

By the way, this is just as true for ANY travel experience — whether you're travelling light or not.

By planning your vacation or holiday far in advance, you not only help travel with less but also enjoy it for longer. Discussing your upcoming trip with friends, family, and colleagues can also allow them to share stories and photos from their travels to your planned destination, mention items you could borrow, or share tips on how to make the most of your next adventure.

Especially when travelling with children, planning and discussing your holiday in advance brings added excitement and enjoyment. Simple activities like researching your destinations, reading books or watching movies set in the places you'll visit, or sampling local foods before departure can enrich both your travel experience and your children's. And, of course, those experiences can help you pack and travel light. Once you have researched and got your kids on board (whether through reading or watching a movie or two), the whole family will better understand what items to include in your pared-down luggage.

Set an intention for your trip

Whilst I always create a detailed spreadsheet with information on where we will be staying, travel times, and suggested activities for each day, the bigger thing that we need to explore when planning our family holidays is less about the sights we will see and more about our *intention* for the trip.

For example, is it adventure, inspiration, relaxation, creating wonderful memories, education, a combination of all of these or something else entirely?

These intentions and associated outcomes require planning.

- Once we have worked out our overall intention for the trip, we can focus on what we will be doing each day.
- From there, we can determine what type of clothing and accessories we may require.

Simply put, which museum we will visit at what time, and the specifics of who's going to wear what on which day, are not the first things we should consider when planning a trip with our children.

Planning

When we are travelling, it's normal to think that planning is all about how we are going to visit all the places we want to see within the time we have available. Naturally, for most of us, travel planning usually involves checking flight timetables, hotel booking rates, and museum schedules to ensure we can plan our days to maximise our sightseeing and enjoyment.

In these situations, planning your clothes often feels like an afterthought, and something you might do the day before or morning of your departure.

However, that sounds very stressful, especially with children of any age.

Advance planning of your clothing and accessory choices, for yourself and your children, means you can be packed and confident days before your departure, minimising the stress of the night before or the day of travel.

Additionally, planning your wardrobe and packing light allows you to be more in the moment while on your holiday or vacation. Rather than worrying about what to wear today, with such a limited selection, the decision is easy. This gives you more time and energy to explore the museums, galleries, palaces, and gardens you have been looking forward to seeing for weeks, months, or even years.

Which is also true for children. Rather than needing to add 'get the kids dressed' to your morning to-do list, before you can all bundle out of wherever you are staying and head out on your first sightseeing expedition of the day, the kids can dress themselves. When there are limited options that all work together as outfits, there is no need for parents to be involved. This approach gives the kids independence while also streamlining the process. No time or energy is lost, nor is there angst about getting up and out into the day. Getting dressed becomes a non-event and a non-issue.

After all, when we travel with our children, it's all about having fun and creating magical memories, not about who wore what.

'Mostly prepared'

Many of us, myself included, were raised with the idea that we should always be prepared. Whether we were Girl Scouts or Boy Scouts or not, many of us grew up in a time when being prepared for all eventualities was part of the culture and society. Our parents or grandparents may have instilled this approach in us, or we may have absorbed it through the news, popular culture, and the daily reminders we saw all around us.

Certainly, this is the case for me. My parents still travel with more belongings than we do.

Yet the 'always be prepared' approach to travelling and packing is not actually beneficial. It often means we end up with far too much luggage, which we struggle to manoeuvre and manage on our own.

My best example of this comes from my personal experience. As mentioned (*see Chapter 1*), when I travelled to the UK by myself at 18 to live and work for a year, I had approximately 50 kilograms of luggage. I couldn't manage all three bags on my own.

This example, along with the other experiences shared earlier, is why I now recommend a 'mostly prepared' approach to packing for travel.

There will be items you know you are likely to use or need on your trip, depending on its duration. Weigh these items, literally. Pop them on a scale and see how heavy they are, then reassess how likely you are to need them.

'Mostly prepared' is how we try to live our lives, too. And so it is no different when we travel. We do not need to cover every single possible circumstance. Instead, we can adjust, make do and, if necessary, practice in the location we are visiting.

Simple things to assist with this mostly prepared approach include having items of clothing that can do double duty or perform multiple tasks. For example, a large scarf can serve as a wrap, a blanket on the plane, a head cover, a colourful accessory, a makeshift cardigan, or a cover-up.

EXAMPLE:

Raincoats. We knew there would likely be wet days when travelling through the US at Christmas. We also knew that travelling through the UK in April would also have wet days. However, we chose not to carry additional raincoats/rain jackets for either trip. Instead, we purchased a cheap poncho in Washington, DC and reused it as needed. In the UK, we managed without raincoats despite having a day or two of rain in the southwest of England. Our jackets got a little damp, and our Stonehenge pictures are very wet indeed, but we coped.

Research

Part of planning involves researching the type of events or locations you will be visiting and checking the weather forecast for that time of year. Knowing whether the weather will be favourable for whatever you plan to do is key to packing light.

In our experience, we have utilised various tools to support this process. Google can help, as can the AccuWeather website, which is reasonably accurate with indicators of average temperatures for previous years. This data has helped us determine the type of weather to expect and the clothing requirements we need to pack.

Additionally, knowing the types of activities you want to undertake plays a significant role in your planning and packing-light preparation. This is pretty straightforward, but to be clear:

- If you plan to spend most of your time with your kids exploring museums, art galleries, and similar places, you'll probably need fewer outdoor clothes and shoes.
- If you plan to walk, hike, or spend long hours outdoors, you will need more outdoor clothing.
- Seasonal variation determines whether this is about sun hats, sun cream, and insect spray, or beanies, gloves, scarves, and thermals.

While taking the time to do detailed planning may seem obvious or even overly organised, it truly is the key to successfully travelling light. Knowing precisely, or as closely as possible, the weather you will encounter ensures you only carry what you need.

Research your accommodation

A quick pre-trip read can help ease the packing anxiety. As well as checking how you access your accommodation (lift or stairs?) and where you'll be sleeping, a thorough read of the listing and reviews can make a huge difference.

For example, it's tempting to pack your own hairdryer, beach or pool towel or coffee maker, but many hotels and Airbnbs provide these essentials, saving you the hassle of bringing them back home. This is especially true for full-service stays. Some Airbnb accommodations (or similar) now offer fully equipped bathrooms with shampoo, conditioner, soap, and towels, along with a well-stocked kitchen featuring coffee and tea-making facilities, oils, vinegar, dressings, and spices.

If the listing doesn't explicitly state what's provided, check the reviews, where you can often learn much more about the accommodation, including its positives and negatives.

The key to travelling light is to carry only what you absolutely need.

More on planning

Whilst these tips do not explicitly relate to packing light, it's part of the travelling light process: plan ahead to maximise enjoyment and ensure ease and flow for all family members.

Choose accommodation wisely

Yes, I've said it a few times already, but it's worth repeating. The gorgeous apartment with a stunning view over the street is odds-on located on an upper floor. Before you fall in love with the view, check the access. Is there a lift, or will you need to use the stairs? Think about this not only for accessing and leaving with your luggage, but also for how you'll manage if your child is tired or unwell and needs to be carried up the stairs, or if you're exhausted after a full day of sightseeing.

One of the reasons travellers generally prefer a centrally located accommodation is because of the ease of popping in and out during the day, especially if you're travelling in a destination where everything closes for several hours after lunch, or if your child (or you) needs an afternoon nap. A lift or stairs will feel more important in these circumstances, and can significantly impact the enjoyment and ease of your experience.

EXAMPLE:

After a full day of travelling, we arrived at our Parisian apartment to discover that the tiny, antiquated lift was out of order. We needed to get ourselves, our luggage and two very tired children (then aged 5 and 9) up sixteen flights of almost spiral stairs, to the eighth floor. We were pleased that our luggage was small and light. During our four-day stay, the lift remained out of service.

Allow for playtime

When planning your itinerary or even just the next day while travelling with children, include time for activities they enjoy, as well as those you do.

So, if they love running around and playing on the playground, be sure to allow time for it. But equally, allow time to visit that museum or gallery you have been desperate to see. If you are planning a big day of walking, do it either the day before or after a travel day, that is, when you'll be mostly in transit and, therefore, spend much of the day sitting. These minor tweaks can ensure everyone has a happy, adventurous trip and feels they get exactly what they wish for from the travel experience.

Wherever possible, balancing the needs of transport travel days with cultural, sporting, and/or natural highlights will allow the whole family to enjoy their trip far more.

EXAMPLE 1:

After spending nearly ten hours in the car driving from San Diego to Las Vegas (due to heavy traffic), and the next day driving from Las Vegas to the Grand Canyon, we decided to spend our day in the Grand Canyon simply walking along the rim. It was minus ten degrees Celsius, and we had intended to take a helicopter trip over the Canyon. But after all that time cooped up in the car, the kids (and adults, too) just needed some time in nature, getting our bodies moving. Looking back on our trip, that was a highlight.

EXAMPLE 2:

Similarly, the day we flew home to Australia from San Francisco, we spent many happy hours at Muir Woods doing extensive walks through the beautiful redwood forest. This meant that by the time we arrived at the airport that evening, we were satisfyingly tired and had had a good dose of fresh air, time in nature, and exercise. We (almost) welcomed the fifteen-hour flight home.

Planning — How we do it

Here is a summary of the key steps we take when planning our next trip with the intention of travelling light. Note that this is not a comprehensive 'to-do' list before travel. Instead, it is specifically for packing and travelling with a smaller bag and fewer items.

Below are the questions we use to help us plan and research each trip. Some of these will seem obvious, and others may be new to you.

Overall Trip details

- Where are we going? (i.e. continent, country, state or region, city)
- How long is the entire trip? (i.e. duration)

Accommodation considerations

- How long will we spend in each location (i.e. number of nights spent in each area or number of nights spent in each accommodation)?
- What style of accommodation are we using?
- How do we access that accommodation? (i.e. is there a reception, a unique code, do we have to meet a host, is there a lift or stairs? Or both?)
- Will there be access to washing facilities in any of our accommodation choices?
- Do we need to adjust some of our choices to ensure that we have access to washing facilities at least once a week? (dependent upon the trip duration)

```
SANITY SAVER TIP:
Check and double-check your accommodation, as sometimes even
when a lift is listed in the details, it might not be
operational. If that's the case, you'll need to climb the
stairs. In such situations, you'll be grateful for smaller,
lighter luggage!
```

Destination details

- Where specifically are we going? (state, city, town, other location details)
- What time of year/season is it?
- What are the average temperatures and weather conditions for each destination?

Trip / Vacation Style

- What type of trip do we want to have? (i.e. relaxing, adventurous, etc.)
- What are the main things we will be doing each day on this trip? (break it down into different activities as necessary)

Further Examples

EXAMPLE 1

- We participated in various activities during our trip to the USA, from hiking in the freezing desert winter at the Grand Canyon to visiting Disneyland in LA, as well as exploring museums and monuments in Washington, DC. These required slightly different packing assessments. In Washington, DC, days were spent primarily in heated buildings. In contrast, the Grand Canyon days were spent primarily outdoors, walking in the freezing wind and trying to avoid slipping on black ice. Knowing how we wanted to spend our time influenced what we chose to pack, particularly our shoe choices (leather or solid-rubber soles) and layers (lots of them, with natural merino wool preferred).

EXAMPLE 2

· During our trip to Europe and Asia, we engaged in a variety of activities and encountered significant variations in weather conditions. We would therefore need clothes that breathe well in the hot, humid conditions of Asia, while also being suitable to wear as a layer in the cooler weather of Europe in April. Therefore, items suitable for all conditions were essential. Long-sleeved cotton shirts were a key item for the males, and a dress I could wear in either cool or warm weather was added to my packing list.

EXAMPLE 3

· We mostly stayed in a resort on our Fiji trip, with most daily activities water- or beach-based. The weather was hot, very humid, and wet. Yet we wanted to go on hikes and celebrate a special occasion while we were away. The beaches were made of coral and were sharp underfoot. Evaluating all these factors, we packed three pairs of shoes each: sports/sneakers for hiking and the flights, sandals or dressed-up slides (depending on gender) for the evening. And then water shoes, also known as aqua socks, for wearing on boats, kayaking, and beach walks.

Make it happen. Your actions:

- Contemplate when your trip is — have you started planning already? If not, today is a good day to start.
- Using the approach shared above as a guide, note down all the details and plans in a single place as you work through your planning list. You may wish to use a notebook and paper, the notes app on your device, or, like me, a spreadsheet.
- Discuss the details and plans with your travel companions, either your partner, friend or children.
- If you're unsure, remember author and podcaster Kendra Adachi's sage advice, and ask yourself: **What can I do now to make things easier later?** Good planning definitely makes things easier later.
- Remember to have fun! Planning is part of looking forward to your holiday.

This chapter aimed to help you understand the importance of planning, not just for your trip, but also for your packing choices. Next, I'll share some additional tips for travelling light.

7

Travelling Light Tips

*"A mind that is stretched by a new experience can never go back
to its old dimensions."*
– Oliver Wendell Holmes

Tip #1 — Select your Airlines wisely

When possible and if your budget allows, consider flying with a full-service airline. Even if you aren't checking luggage, the advantages of having a full-service airline are significant when travelling with children. Meals, activities, games, and movies are all provided. Which means you don't need to bring any entertainment for you or your children on the plane, because it is all taken care of, including snacks, too!

Plus, if you need to check luggage (perhaps on your way home because you've purchased a lot of Lego — true story), you can do so without incurring additional costs.

Tip #2 —Choose a colour scheme

Choose a colour scheme for the clothes you will pack. Either do this as part of your planning and preparation, or while you are laying out items before packing. And yes, this tip applies to ALL family members.

When the shirt you want to wear coordinates with the trousers, which in turn match the jumper (sweater), you not only look more put together but also find that clothing selection is made easier. When a few of these items are favourites (see below), packing light becomes more achievable.

It's also easier for children to dress themselves quickly when they know whatever clothing they put on will coordinate.

Plus, washing matters less when everything coordinates with everything else or at least tonally matches, as each shirt or top goes with each pair of trousers/jeans/pants/skirt.

Tip #3 — Pack a few favourite items

Yes, packing a few of your favourite clothing items can make the difference between a successful trip with carry-on-only luggage and one that never feels quite right. I genuinely believe the size of your wardrobe (or bag) has nothing to do with style. It is possible to look stylish and still travel light.

Why this tip? Because packing a favourite item or two for your trip makes you feel like yourself. It also makes dressing each day easier, as you will feel good wearing the item. Implementing this tip helps alleviate some of the need for options while also addressing the desire for a choice based on how you feel that day.

Intuitive dressing is great at home, but adds unnecessary weight and bulk when attempting to travel light. Having one or two favourite items means you can still dress to make yourself feel good without needing to pack multiple additional items.

However, I don't recommend packing favourite items unless they meet the following criteria:

- You love it.
- It makes you feel and look good.
- It suits the activities and climate where you will be travelling.
- It washes and dries easily.
- It coordinates with the rest of your travel wardrobe.

However, if your favourite item meets one of the following, DO NOT pack it.

- It's a family heirloom.
- It is not easily replaced.
- It's made of delicate fabric.
- It's heavy and will take an extended time to dry.
- It's dry-clean only (and is not an outer layer, like a coat).

If you have identified a favourite item that meets the first list but not the second, and you still really want to take it, add it to your list for consideration and review later.

Tip #4 — Avoid rain gear, if possible

We recommend packing a light rain jacket if you *know* you will be somewhere where rain is likely; however, we do not generally recommend packing rain gear.

Firstly, single-purpose rain jackets can be heavy and take up a lot of space. Secondly, an umbrella, even a small pocket-sized one, can add weight and actually provide very little protection from the rain.

Instead, we recommend showerproof jackets, such as down jackets for warmth, with an additional showerproof coating, which most have.

EXAMPLE 1:

In the USA and the UK, we experienced wet weather. In both instances, we managed to do so without carrying dedicated rain protection items. In the US, our days in Washington, D.C., were marked by torrential rain. Instead of letting it slow us down, we purchased clear rain ponchos for a few dollars (US$2.50 each) for all of us. Yes, we looked a little odd, but they did the job. Afterwards, the ponchos dried in the hotel room overnight and were ready to be used the following day. We kept the ponchos for New York (our next destination), but didn't need to use them again. For a total of US$10 (about A$15 at the time), we had two full days of rain protection without needing to carry a rain jacket or umbrella for the other 20 days of our travel.

EXAMPLE 2:

In the UK, we had only one day of proper rain, which coincided with our visit to Stonehenge. We managed to still sightsee by juggling our time. So, instead of going straight to see the famous stones, we spent some time in the museum section. Once the rain eased to a drizzle, we could head over to the monument and marvel at the wonder of Stonehenge. It was a minor adjustment and in no way altered our enjoyment of the activity, but once again it saved us from carrying rain gear when we were travelling with less than 7 kilograms each.

Tip #5 — Scarves

Ladies, this one is for you, and perhaps your daughters as well. Scarves of various weights are perfect for intuitive dressers seeking variety in their outfits, providing options without unnecessary weight or bulk. They are also ideal for adding colour, variation, warmth, and/or sun protection. Plus, they generally roll up small and weigh very little. And they don't usually need to be washed!

As a bonus, scarves can be doubled up for extra warmth if needed.

EXAMPLE 1:

In New York City, when it was below zero outside, I wore a small cotton scarf for colour (instead of jewellery) and then added a large pashmina-style scarf for extra warmth. I found this tip was particularly useful when we went inside, as I still felt stylish and colour-coordinated, even after removing my coat and large scarf. Larger shawls or pashmina-style scarves can also change the feel of an outfit, depending on how you wear them.

EXAMPLE 2:

Wearing my merino scarf as a shawl or wrap (rather than in a loose knot around my neck) in Paris gave the outfit I had been wearing all day a new look and feel when we headed out for dinner.

EXAMPLE 3:

In Singapore, I used a lightweight poly-cotton large scarf as a sarong when walking between our room and the hotel pool. The same scarf, looped around twice, kept my neck warm on a flight where the air conditioning was too cold.

Tip #6 — Handkerchiefs and Tissues

Use small packs of wet wipes for the plane or to clean up the kids' mess. Also, contemplate packing a few cotton handkerchiefs. They are reusable, wash out easily and can be dampened to clean up messes. They are also an environmentally friendly option. Plus, if a handkerchief stays in a pocket and goes through the washing machine, there is no need to pick tiny bits of tissue off everything or waste time and money rewashing the entire load!

No tissues is especially important when travelling light. You will need to wash at frequent intervals, but you won't want to spend hours in the hotel or apartment rewashing items you have already cleaned to remove all that white tissue. So, consider packing a couple of handkerchiefs per person for your trip. Cotton handkerchiefs are very light and small.

Tip #7 — Laundry

As we've mentioned, to pack light, you need to accept that you'll have to do laundry. When travelling solo or with a partner, washing socks and undergarments in the bathroom sink can be fine. It's easy to use the hand soap or shampoo provided by your accommodation (if available) for this purpose. However, when travelling with your family, there is more laundry to do than when you're on your own, and using the provided soaps can be hard on your hands and may leave your clothing less soft than you'd prefer.

We've travelled with a small plastic container of laundry powder, which worked fine, but our new, preferred choice is laundry sheets. They are easy to carry, weigh almost nothing, and can be cut or torn into small pieces for hand washing or smaller loads in a machine. We love them so much, we use them at home too when we're not travelling!

Laundry sheets were once hard to find, but nowadays, most large supermarkets stock them in the laundry aisle. Depending on how long you're travelling and how often you plan to wash, which may depend on how young or messy your kids are, you might want to take 4-5 or more sheets, stored in a Ziploc or similar waterproof bag. We cut the sheets in half before leaving, and even when taking enough for a few weeks, it ends up being no larger than a few sheets of paper and about the same weight. If we stay somewhere with a machine and need to do a full load, then two half sheets are more than enough—even for smelly teenage boys' clothes!

Tip #8 — Reading material

As a family of avid readers, we must allow for reading material. Ebooks and audiobooks have been a life-changer for us.

If you're into 2-for-1 book deals at the airport (like my husband!), keep reading. The temptation of a new novel is real, but those extra paperbacks can quickly weigh down your luggage. Instead, look into ebooks to enjoy a good read without sacrificing weight or space.

Either utilise your local library service, which lends ebooks, or check out the latest releases on your preferred platform before your flight.

For maximum convenience, we suggest downloading ebooks in advance to your Kindle, iPad, smartphone, or other device at home before you leave.

Audiobooks are also an excellent resource for keeping kids happy when driving or travelling by other means. We have found that audiobooks are great for kids and adults alike. We have used Audible (via Amazon) and a service called BorrowBox, which we access through our local library, which lends audiobook downloads for 2 or 3 weeks. With a good story or two to listen to and eBooks to read, we each have options for how we wish to enjoy our reading material, which are also transport-friendly.

> *"Only pack light things, not heavy things, like big books or*
> *heavy toys!"*
> *— Nick, age 6*

Tip #9 — Pre-Book

We like to book ahead whenever possible. That means pre-booking accommodation, transport, and even admission to galleries and museums. We have found this to be efficient and economical.

These days, it is easy to pre-book many of these things online. In addition, the advent of e-tickets and smartphone scanners supports travelling light. There's no need to carry a hefty folder of paper; nearly everything can be done via phone.

Another reason we like to pre-book tickets is that waiting in line is not particularly enjoyable when travelling with children. At times, that is an understatement. A three- or four-hour queue to get into a location becomes an absolute nightmare when your child is bored beyond belief, tired, hungry, and likely to need to use the toilet.

It's much easier to have pre-booked admission and walk straight in. Then you can see what you've been planning and are excited to see, and leave again. In the time you would've spent queuing and waiting, you have been, seen, and are done.

BONUS — kid-specific tips from our boys for other children

Toiletries

For kids, toiletries should be stored in a clear plastic container, such as a Ziploc bag or a purpose-made/purchased zippered pouch, which makes it easier to find your toiletries when it's dark, early, or when you are just feeling tired.

Safety

Ensure you always stay close to one of your parents. Otherwise, you might get lost, and you won't be able to get through security. Plus, it's scary when you get lost.

Gratitude

Always be helpful to your parents, as they planned this incredible trip for you.

Be adventurous with food

When given the opportunity, try new food, especially when you're overseas, and take advantage of well-known local specialities. It's fun to try new foods, and you might even discover a new favourite dish!

"The favourites I tried when travelling include black-eyed pea soup, catfish and chips, a Sally Lunn bun, chocolate crêpes, and chocolate croissants."
— Nick, age 6

Make it happen. Your actions:

- If you've not booked your trip yet, prioritise full-service airlines that provide meals, entertainment, and luggage check-in without extra fees, especially when travelling with children.
- Select a colour scheme for your clothing and your kids' to simplify outfit choices and ensure every item matches, making packing and dressing easier.
- Assess carefully whether you pack any favourite items.

· Opt for versatile layers, especially for outerwear.

This chapter provided some tips aimed to help you adjust to and enjoy travelling with less. In the next chapter, I explore additional tips for making these switches more sustainable.

8

How to Travel Light in a More Sustainable Way

"Take only memories, leave only footprints."
– Chief Seattle

I'm aware that environmental factors are a key reason many of us choose to travel with less. Indeed, travelling with a smaller, carry-on-only bag lightens how much you personally carry and also has significant environmental benefits.

When you pack light and limit your luggage to carry-on size, or as required by some airlines, to seven kilograms or less, you reduce the overall weight on the plane, which means less fuel is used during your flight. Since air travel is one of the more challenging modes of transport to make environmentally friendly, this reduction in fuel usage is a crucial advantage of travelling light.

Here are some practical tips for maintaining a sustainable travel routine while keeping your luggage to a minimum.

Invest in Reusable Items

Instead of buying plastic water bottles at the airport and then again at your destination, use reusable ones. Additionally, acquiring a clear, envelope-style reusable bag, similar to a Ziploc bag, for toiletries could be a valuable investment.

Using a portable cutlery set instead of disposable plastic utensils allows you to enjoy meals on the go without contributing to waste. This tip may not be relevant for you and your family, depending on your destination, accommodation plans, and travel style.

Utilise handkerchiefs instead of tissues to further reduce waste (*see Tip #6, Chapter 7*)

Review Toiletries

Use small, travel-sized refillable bottles filled with your favourite products, or opt for products with zero or minimal packaging to reduce single-use plastic. You can also reduce the size of your toiletries by only taking what you need. Many travel-sized toiletries are still bigger than we will need for the duration of the trip. Cutting a wedge from your preferred bar or soap, or decanting into a smaller container, is a sustainability win, and good for your weight limit too.

Pack Light Clothing

Bring versatile outfits that can be easily mixed and matched, are physically lightweight, and can be washed and dried each night. Ideally, choose clothing made from sustainable materials and or fabrics that can be washed and dried easily. Jeans are okay because, generally, you'll be wearing them, and they require infrequent washing. However, anything close to your body, like undergarments, T-shirts, socks and so on, should be able to be washed by hand and dried overnight.

By keeping your clothing items physically lighter and utilising layers when needed, you can keep your luggage lightweight and environmentally friendly.

Use What You Have

Use items you already own as much as possible, for clothing, accessories and extras. Look at borrowing or renting things you need only for the trip (like specific bags or gear you won't use again). Aim to reduce your packing down to the bare essentials to reduce weight.

Hand Washing Only When Necessary

Airing clothes worn as a layer (not next to the body) is often all that is required and can be done easily in a hotel or hostel room.

If you need to wash clothes, do it by hand only when necessary to save water and energy, and air-dry. As a bonus, it's better for your clothes too if they are washed less frequently.

Better Transportation Choices

Choose trains, buses or ferries over planes for short trips, as they generally have a lower carbon footprint. And as a bonus, when you factor in the time required to travel to the airport, check in and wait, as well as the travel time at the other end, for short trips, alternate methods of transport can end up being faster and more economical too.

Pre-book and choose electronic

Pre-book your travel and other activities to minimise the need for paper or guidebooks, and embrace digital tickets and guides on your smartphone or tablet.

Support Local Artisans

If you decide to purchase souvenirs, consider buying from local artists rather than mass-produced items, as this will help support the local economy and reduce transportation-related emissions.

Make it happen. Your actions:

- Review your current go-to travel bag and evaluate switching to a smaller, carry-on-sized option that meets airline weight and size requirements.
- As a minimum, consider investing in a clear, TSA-approved, reusable toiletry bag to minimise single-use plastics.
- Choose versatile, lightweight clothing made from sustainable materials that can be mixed and matched. Pack only the essentials to keep your luggage light and manageable.
- Plan transportation and activities. Opt for eco-friendly transportation like trains or buses for short trips, and pre-book travel and activities digitally to reduce paper waste.

Many of these tips have been briefly referenced elsewhere in the book. But by integrating the tips in this chapter and in this book into your travel plans, you can enjoy the freedom and excitement of travelling light while minimising your environmental impact.

Now that I've covered mindset, planning and shared some tips for how to make travelling with less, achievable and even enjoyable, next we are getting down to business — we are starting to actually pack.

III

Make it happen! Practicalities

"Start where you are. Use what you have. Do what you can."
– Arthur Ashe

9

Travel Bags to Lighten the Load

"Let your memory be your travel bag."
- Aleksandr Solzhenitsyn

Bag choice is key for travelling with less, especially when travelling with children. Your bags form a natural boundary or container for the amount you can physically bring and carry, which is why selecting the right weight and style for your planned trip is crucial.

After all, no matter what size bag you decide on, you'll end up filling it. It's how humans primarily operate; we see an empty space and have a strong desire to fill it.

My brother was the first one to really drive this point home to me, yet I ignored it. Which was why I ended up with a massive eighty-litre (80L) backpack for a six-week trip, and could barely lift and carry it on my back. He'd warned me that whatever size bag I chose, I'd fill it. He was right. (*Mike, if you're reading this — here it is in print; You. Were. Right.*)

All that's to say, bag selection can really make or break your travel experience, even when you're not travelling carry-on only. But when you are, it's even more imperative to get it right.

Before our first carry-on-only overseas trip, I conducted extensive research on luggage. What travel bag or bags would suit our needs? What did others recommend?

I found a lot of data on the best travel bags, but it was all aimed at single adults.

The few articles and posts I found about suitable travel bags for children were not particularly helpful for my kids' ages (then four and seven years old). Certainly, there were some great suggestions about toddler bags (the Trunki is so cute!), but nothing my boys would have been happy to be seen with, nor that would continue to work for our family as the children grew.

After weeks of research, I purchased a backpack for myself. I returned it a couple of weeks later and exchanged it for a Samsonite wheeled bag. Since then, my husband has used that bag for his work trips, and I've received a 'hand-me-down' bag from my parents. The bag I use most often now is a small wheeled laptop bag that converts to a backpack. Although I've never used it like that, partly because it seems like a good idea in theory, but in practice, the wheels are uncomfortable against my spine.

All that's to say, you don't need me to tell you exactly what bag to use or purchase. But I will share with you the questions I asked myself, my husband, and the kids to determine what type of bag or bags would suit us.

Questions to ask yourself before you determine what luggage you need:

- Where are we travelling to? (country, location)
- How are we getting there? (air, train, bus)
- What airline (if applicable) are we flying?
- What restrictions do we need to take into account based on our transport? (i.e. airline size/weight restrictions, train size/weight restrictions)
- What type of accommodation do we intend to use? (hotels, self-contained apartments, B&Bs, hostels, camping)
- Where is that accommodation? (centrally located, near transport, further afield?)
- What is the access like for that accommodation? (lift, stairs)
- What kind of transportation will we most likely be using once we arrive? (taxi, Uber, hire car, public transport – bus, rail, ferry, organised tour, bicycle)
- What are we doing there? (activities – hiking, sightseeing, museums, galleries, shopping, theme parks)

While these questions may feel overly detailed, they are important to contemplate. We also considered them in Chapter 6 to gain insight into your overall planning.

SANITY SAVER TIP:
In case of recent changes, double-check the specifications and dimensions of carry-on and personal items for each transport type again a week before you leave.

How we do it

We select our luggage using the above questions and going into as much detail as possible.

Size and Weight

This is important. Airlines and trains have detailed requirements regarding the size and/or weight of your bag.

Do your research!

I can't emphasise this enough.

Google your airline or airlines and their specific restrictions, then check several other posts appearing in the search results, ideally from a variety of sources, including other travellers. This may feel excessive, but please ensure you do this, as each airline has slightly different requirements. The interpretation of these requirements can vary as well, which is where reading posts from other frequent travellers, not just the airline's page, can help clarify how the requirements are enforced.

Some have weight restrictions but no size limits, while others have strict size/dimensions limits but appear less concerned about the weight of your bag or bags.

Also, check the requirements for any internal transportation you will be using, including domestic airlines, trains, ferries, and buses. It may surprise you that trains in Europe can also have strict luggage limits. Domestic airlines also vary worldwide, from a five-kilogram limit to quite large weight and size limits.

EXAMPLE 1:

We flew American Airlines codeshare with Qantas on our trip to the USA. International flights had different requirements than domestic flights, since we were on a Qantas aircraft. At that time, Qantas based its requirements on overall dimensions, whereas American Airlines used specific measurements that all bags had to comply with.

SANITY SAVER TIP:
When unsure, use a bag that complies with the smallest measurements for ALL the transport you'll use during your entire trip.

EXAMPLE 2:

When we travelled to the UK, Europe, and Singapore, we flew with Singapore Airlines. They operate with a weight limit for carry-on luggage. Dimensions are important, but not as important as weight. Each bag, regardless of its size, is weighed. All bags must be seven kilograms or less.

SANITY SAVER TIP:
Always check the exact specifications of the airline you are travelling with, as variations in application and interpretation are wide.

EXAMPLE 3:

On our trip to Western Australia, we flew Jetstar, one of Australia's budget airlines. They operate with a weight limit for all carry-on luggage. Dimensions are important, but not as critical as weight. The total of all items for each person is weighed. Yes, your personal items and luggage are weighed together to determine the total. And the total weight of ALL bags for each individual must be seven kilograms or less.

Based on this, our boys each swapped out their usual bags for lighter-weight duffel-style bags that weighed less than their usual travel bags, meaning they could still bring their various devices, headphones, and chargers, which, as teens, they deemed more essential than some of their clothing.

SANITY SAVER TIP:
Weigh your bag empty before you start packing, as this will
give you an idea of the maximum weight you can carry. This
is important, as a small bag can weigh more than 7 kilograms
depending on its contents, especially if it has a frame and
wheels. Adjust your bag choice if necessary (based on the
weight of your clothes/shoes).

EXAMPLE 4:

Our trip to Fiji included two flights in a tiny plane, on which not only the luggage but also we were weighed! In this case, ALL luggage except for very small backpacks or handbags was placed in the hold.

Use your personal item

When you check your airline's website for details regarding their carry-on restrictions, note what they define as a 'personal item'. Many airlines allow a 'personal item' in addition to a carry-on bag. Most airlines define a personal item as a bag that fits under the seat in front of you; however, the size requirements vary by airline or mode of transportation, just as they do for carry-on luggage.

Generally, a personal item could be a small backpack, a woman's handbag/purse, a laptop bag or an umbrella. But please note, your personal item is ONE of these, not all of them together! Utilising your personal item can make a significant difference to your packing plans.

Using this personal item allowance wisely makes packing and luggage choices far easier.

SANITY SAVER TIP:
Most airlines require that personal items be placed under
the seat in front of you, rather than in the overhead
locker. Keep this in mind for long-haul flights, especially

if you or your children intend to use a daypack as your
personal item and prefer ample legroom.

EXAMPLE 1:

I frequently use a mid-sized leather handbag that converts to a backpack as my personal item. It contains my wallet, passport, toiletries, iPhone, earbuds, a pocket pack of tissues, make-up and toiletries bag, pen, and the like. PLUS items for the children: passports and hand wipes. When we reach our destination, this bag becomes the one I use every day when we are out and about, whether sightseeing or hiking.

EXAMPLE 2:

My husband uses a small cycling daypack as his personal item. It contains his SLR camera and camera bag, wallet, passport, book, hand wipes, toiletries, pocket pack of tissues, and other such items. It's also been used to carry an additional pair of shoes and/or his jacket (rolled up small). Similarly, my husband uses this small daypack as his everyday bag when we arrive at our destination, swapping out toiletries for snacks and water bottles for himself and the kids.

Luggage and kids

After reviewing all the questions, planning and thinking, we also asked the kids what luggage or bag they would like to use. Asking them and then allowing them to decide helps ensure they are happy with the choice and instils a sense of accountability. We've found they are less likely to complain about carrying or wheeling their bag if they have been actively involved in the selection process.

We use what we already own as much as possible

For our first trip overseas, travelling light, we purchased two new wheeled bags. One was a Samsonite domestic carry-on size (based on dimensions), and the other was a travel laptop bag for our eldest child. My husband, not wanting to miss out, also decided he wanted a new bag and bought himself a leather overnight bag. These new items have been an excellent investment, as we have used them on every overseas trip since 2014 and on numerous domestic adventures.

We also used items we already owned, including day packs, smaller backpacks, a leather handbag, and others.

We think more broadly about luggage and how we will be travelling

When travelling with young children, consider worst-case travel luggage scenarios and plan for these. That may mean determining that, if necessary, you could wheel or carry all the child's luggage if they are too tired or unwell to do so.

EXAMPLE:

Our youngest child was only 4 years old on our first overseas trip, travelling light. We knew there would be a good chance he would sometimes be too tired to be responsible for his bag and may also need to be carried through airports when the flights were late at night.

Knowing this, we chose a wheeled laptop backpack for him (one we already owned). It was a convertible bag with hidden straps that could convert into a backpack if needed. We then purchased a similar bag (in a different colour) for our older son.

We thought that, if necessary, we could convert the children's bags into backpacks for each adult to carry in addition to their own luggage.

I had a wheeled suitcase, and my husband had an overnight bag with a shoulder strap, which meant we would still each have a hand free to hold onto a child.

Choose luggage based on your destination and transportation

As outlined above, the choice of luggage can make or break the experience of travelling light.

Knowing where you are travelling and the transportation you will use can help you and your family choose the best luggage.

EXAMPLES:

USA

On our USA trip, we travelled with three traditional wheeled domestic carry-on-sized bags for the children and me, because we knew the places we intended to stay and visit, such as hotels and airports, would have smooth surfaces for easy mobility.

UK/EUROPE

During our trip to Europe, we utilised a combination of backpacks and wheeled bags, with the latter offering the option to convert into a backpack when needed. We chose this because wheeling bags over cobblestone streets is not a pleasant experience for anyone, and it is particularly challenging when expecting your young child to be responsible for their own bag. Additionally, when staying in hostels and small apartments throughout the UK and Europe, it is often the case that there is no elevator and many stairs to climb. Small wheeled bags and backpacks made carrying our luggage up the narrow stairs easier.

ASIA

In Asia, we stayed in high-end hotels, so wheeled luggage was fine. That said, the older child preferred a backpack because it kept his hands free and offered the added ease of movement that comes with having his bag on his back.

FIJI

In Fiji, we travelled on tiny planes between islands but then stayed in a resort. We used wheeled domestic laptop bags for the youngest child and me, a day-pack-sized backpack for the older child, and a leather overnight bag for my husband.

DOMESTIC AUSTRALIA

We tend to stay in self-contained apartments or similar accommodations, so wheeled luggage is generally fine. As the boys have grown older, they prefer using a small wheeled bag or a soft duffel bag, with a small daypack as their personal item (often used primarily to carry their water bottle, snacks, and technology). As the children have grown older, their choice of bags has changed.

On our more recent domestic trips, our teenage boys have preferred lightweight duffel bags over wheeled bags, valuing the flexibility of a soft-sided bag and its light weight, which allows them to carry their heavy shoes and bulky clothes without difficulty.

This is particularly important when a carry-on limit is strictly enforced, as on budget airlines such as Jetstar in Australia, where the *total weight* of your items must be *below* seven kilograms (see above), including your personal item and hand luggage.

Hard-earned luggage tips

Soft-sided bags

- When possible, choose a soft-sided carry-on bag. While many love hard-shell suitcases, and they have their place, we never use them. Instead, we use soft-sided small 'roll-aboard' cases, a backpack or a soft duffel bag for our carry-on luggage.
- The chances of being separated from your stuff on board are minimised because of this choice: it's much easier to manoeuvre it into an already-crowded overhead locker and, in the event it just won't fit, and if it's small enough, you can usually pop it under the seat in front, especially when travelling with young children who don't need the extra leg room. However, please note that this option is less effective with teenagers. Instead, they tend to have their personal items, including chargers, devices, headphones, and power banks, stashed under the seat in front.

Wheeled bags

- Using a wheeled bag with four wheels might be fine on smooth surfaces. However, even if you organise a direct transfer from the airport or train station to your accommodation, there's a good chance you'll be wheeling your luggage over uneven ground, cobblestones, or bumpy paths when travelling. Or you'll be lugging it up the stairs if the tiny, old lift in the beautiful historic apartment you're staying in is out of service. If a backpack-style bag isn't suitable, consider investing in a two-wheeled roll-aboard bag. They are harder to find these days, but handle cobblestones much better than the four-wheel versions, and are easier to manoeuvre.

```
SANITY SAVER TIP:
Check how you will access your chosen accommodation and
choose your luggage accordingly. Large hotels usually have
lifts, while smaller boutique hotels in historic parts of
town might not. City apartments, such as those on Airbnb,
often lack lifts. If the listing doesn't explicitly state
whether there are stairs or a lift, read the reviews from
other travellers.
```

When out and about

- Avoid large backpacks when walking around cities to stay safe and avoid looking like a tourist. For men, a small backpack might be okay. A crossbody bag or a small handbag-sized backpack is preferable for women.
- Alternatively, if you're wearing a jacket, streamline your belongings to only what you can fit in your pockets. We did this at Disneyland—carrying a wallet, hotel room key, phone, handkerchief, and for me, a tinted lip saver (it was very cold and windy). Everything else, like passports, was locked in the hotel safe.

Make it happen. Your actions:

- Consider your trip duration and destination.
- Reflect on the transport you will be using.
- Determine the type of accommodation you will be using.
- Take a moment to assess the luggage you already own.
- Review your bag options based on your existing choices.
- Measure and weigh each bag, as required.

- If necessary, ask family or friends if they have a small bag you could borrow.
- Select a 'trial' bag for each family member.

After completing these actions, you should have a reasonable idea of the dimensions and space you are working with. Next, we'll look at filling it with your clothes, accessories and other required items. First, though, I'll explore how you can streamline and reduce your toiletries. Toiletries and liquids are often a stumbling block when attempting to travel light, so I'll address them next.

10

Toiletries and Other Messy Things

"How subtle is the relationship between the traveller and his luggage! He knows, as no one else knows, its idiosyncrasies, its contents ... and always some small nuisance which he wishes he had not brought; had known, indeed, before starting that he would regret it, but brought it all the same."
— *Vita Sackville-West*

It may seem unnecessary to dedicate an entire chapter to toiletries and other messy items. Still, we have found that packing them correctly can make all the difference when you have limited space and weight.

Let's get the basics right up front.

TSA and Airline liquid restrictions mean you must be *very* disciplined about the amount and size of liquids you bring.

The travel-size items are great, but they are often too big for what you really need.

The key to remember is that if you are travelling carry-on only, you are constrained by the TSA liquids allowance on most international flights. All liquid items must be one hundred millilitres (100ml) or less and carried in a clear quart-sized bag (equivalent to a one-litre size).

Toiletries

Packing toiletries is not as much of an issue for children as it is for adults, simply because kids generally don't have or need as much stuff. They often only need a toothbrush, some toothpaste, and maybe a special body wash or deodorant (depending on age).

For adults, teenagers and older children, it's different. We often have a range of personal care, grooming, hair care, and makeup products.

The key to remember is that every person in your family can, and should, have their own toiletries bag with their items, which helps with the TSA regulations. But it also ensures you aren't all without toothpaste if one person loses their toiletries bag. Additionally, if you find that, as a family, you are seated separately on the plane (as we have been nearly every time!), then each child having their own toiletries makes after-meal teeth brushing a little easier for the parent responsible for that child.

Other Messy Things

Most of your liquids are likely to be toiletries or makeup, but you may also have liquid medications and want to bring laundry detergent for washing clothes.

For liquid medications, ask your pharmacist or healthcare provider if they can offer solid forms or pre-measured doses, such as pills or patches. Certainly, if your child cannot swallow pills (as one of mine can't), you can often request a smaller version of the medication.

Instead of liquid laundry detergent, experiment with laundry detergent sheets or capsules, which are compact and travel-friendly.

How we do it

For toiletries and all other messy things, we use the Three Ss:

- Streamline,
- Substitution, and
- Smaller

Streamline

First, examine the toiletry items you deem necessary. Scrutinise whether each item is truly essential.

The aim is to streamline down to only the items you *actually* need, not just the things you think you need.

As mentioned in the Planning Chapter (*Chapter 6*), consider the type of travel you are undertaking and where you will be staying. For example, for most places where you are staying, soaps, shampoo, conditioner, and body lotion may be provided. In that case, you can avoid packing these items unless you have allergies or particularly sensitive skin.

Part of streamlining involves assessing whether you need to carry these items with you or if you can purchase them upon arrival at your destination. For example, we do not bring children's (liquid) paracetamol with us on our travels, as we knew that, should we require it, generally we can buy it at our destination, which we had to do in Washington, DC. And it was fine. It's more efficient to purchase specific items as needed to save space and weight, rather than carrying them around unnecessarily.

Substitution

After considering your essential items, you should also ascertain where you can substitute. Toiletries swaps include:

- Micellar water instead of makeup remover and cleanser
- Stick deodorant, or paste instead of spray or roll-on
- Toothpaste tablets instead of a tube of toothpaste

EXAMPLE 1:

I switch to facial cleansing wipes when travelling instead of using a cream face wash as I do at home. These wipes are not liquids, so they can be stored elsewhere in my bag without needing to be placed in my clear TSA bag. Which in turn allows more space in the TSA bag for things I'd prefer not to substitute, such as face cream.

Substitutions also make a big difference for makeup. Possible makeup swaps include:

- Pencil eyeliner instead of liquid eyeliner
- Pencil lip liner instead of lipstick
- Moisturising tinted lip balm instead of lip gloss/lipstick
- Pressed powder foundation instead of liquid foundation

EXAMPLE 2:

Instead of using a facial moisturiser, sun cream, and foundation (all of which I use at home), when travelling, I opt for a single product that replaces these three: a BB or CC cream. This type of cream works well for me, as it means one small squeeze tube rather than three large ones.

Smaller

Use smaller versions of your preferred brand for the liquid items you absolutely must have (like toothpaste and deodorant). Most supermarkets, pharmacies, and drug stores have a travel section where smaller versions of everyday toiletries are stocked.

You can decant these into smaller containers for larger items, such as body wash or your preferred shampoo, if you need to bring specific products due to skin sensitivities or allergies.

Remember, if you are bringing them, shared items such as body wash or shampoo can be placed in your child's TSA (Ziploc) bag.

A note about toiletry bags

We own many terrific toiletry bags, including those with special pockets, zip-out sections, clear plastic sections, mesh sections, and other features. They are all lovely to use.

However, we NEVER use them for international travel when travelling carry-on only. There are three reasons why we don't use them.

1. They generally weigh more and take up more space than we are prepared to give to toiletries.
2. The correctly sized Ziploc bag removes doubt. We know the bag is precisely the size permitted. It weighs almost nothing and can be easily squeezed into a handbag or other 'personal item'.
3. A Ziploc or reusable lightweight wipe-down bag is easily cleaned or replaced if spills occur inside.

Additionally, when travelling internationally with carry-on only luggage, items deemed liquids, such as creams, must be placed in a Ziploc-sized bag and removed for security screening. Remember that non-liquid items can be carried in a separate section of your main bag, not the Ziploc. For example, if you choose to use facial wipes instead of a liquid cleanser, you can stow them elsewhere in your bag and do not need to include them in your TSA bag.

Make it happen. Your actions:

- Consider the length of your trip, your destination, and the type or types of accommodation you will be using to determine the toiletries and personal items you will need.
- Review all personal care items to determine if they are essential and necessary or 'nice to have'.
- Review your current collection of travel-sized and other toiletries to avoid purchasing duplicates or unnecessary items.
- Focus on packing minimal liquids and creams, and look at swaps to non-liquid formats where possible.
- Measure and weigh all your essential toiletries and adjust where needed to smaller-sized containers.
- For essential liquids and creams, downsize to the smallest size possible.
- Allocate an approved-size Ziploc bag for each family member to test-fit and organise.
- Complete a trial pack of toiletries (and makeup if applicable) for all family members.

Now that I've walked you through how to minimise and pack toiletries and other messy items, next, I'll briefly cover the extras that we often think our kids need when they are away from home.

11

Kids' Toys, Entertainment and 'Just In Case' Items

" 'Just in case' is the curse of packing."
– Alexandra Potter

Many parents I spoke to expressed hesitation about travelling with less simply because they were concerned about keeping their children entertained, and had grown accustomed to packing an entire carry-on-size bag full of toys and games for their child.

Alternatively, they were concerned with 'what if' scenarios, leading to a substantial amount of space taken up with 'just in case' items.

Toys and Entertainment

As with every item we pack, it's essential to determine what we truly need and how our children prefer to be entertained.

A small notebook, a pencil, or a pen may be sufficient for keeping a travel journal. Other children may prefer a selection of coloured pencils and a colouring book.

Once again, preparation, thinking and planning are vital. Consider the type of travel you will be undertaking, the duration of your trip, and what you plan to do once you reach your destination.

A key thing to remember is that nearly all airlines (especially full-service airlines) will provide some form of entertainment for your small child. In addition to movies and in-seat screen entertainment, the airline's non-screen entertainment often includes its own set of coloured pencils, pencil cases, colouring books, and other resources. Therefore, there is no need to pack these items, as you will acquire them on the first leg of your journey.

That is not to say you need to keep them! Once they have served their purpose, you can recycle, edit, or give them to another child you meet on your way.

Keep in mind the type of trip you are planning. If you are going to a single location where you will all be relaxing for days, your entertainment and toy requirements may differ from those of a family on the move and sightseeing.

In our experience, older children and teenagers really want only their device (such as an iPhone) and headphones. With a movie or two downloaded, or an audio or ebook, their entertainment is contained in one small device.

Just in case items

All of the items below are the things people most frequently pack as 'just in case' to alleviate concerns expressed as 'what if'. Most of these can be swapped or removed with minimal inconvenience.

Including them on this list doesn't mean you *shouldn't* pack them. What it does mean is think carefully about whether you really, genuinely need them or if an alternative option (which you will already have with you, or that you don't need to carry) could be utilised instead.

Of course, in some circumstances, depending on where you are travelling and the type of accommodation you are staying in, some of these items will be necessary. For instance, shampoo and soap are essential when camping or staying in youth hostels, as they are not provided. And, a better-equipped medical kit and a small sewing kit may be good to have if you are travelling in a remote area. I have marked these items with an asterisk.*

Just in case items you probably don't need:

- Phone, iPad and laptop - do you need all three? Can you streamline?
- Umbrella - generally, they are heavy and don't protect you adequately anyway.
- Raincoat - a lightweight waterproof jacket or shell is more versatile (*see Chapter 6 and Chapter 12 for more*)
- Hairdryer - Most accommodations have one, and if there isn't one in the room, you can often request one.
- Shampoo* - generally provided.
- Conditioner* - generally provided.
- Soap/body wash* - generally provided.
- Sewing kit* - you can often borrow one from reception or source one at your destination.
- Complete medical/medication pain relief kit* - if you or your children have specific needs, such as allergies, or are travelling outside of large towns and cities, this may be necessary. Otherwise, consider what you need to see you through until you can purchase at your destination.
- Any item that you wouldn't need, and if you did, you could get it without too much hassle. E.g. you don't need a whole packet of Band-Aids when maybe two or three will suffice until you can get to a pharmacy to purchase some in your destination.

- Multiple paper books - look at using a device instead. Or, if you prefer to read on paper, take one book with you on your travels, gift it to someone, and purchase another while you are away.
- Washing liquid - swap for non-liquid laundry sheets, which are also smaller and lighter.
- Travel clothesline - use a clothes hanger, or the room/accommodation may have a clothesline or clothes airer.
- Multiple power adapters: a single multi-country adapter can replace them, or you can purchase one in your destination (see example below).

Thorough research and planning (*see Chapter 6*) will help remove the need for the vast majority of these items.

How we do it

Entertainment and toys

When the children were younger, we learned to streamline the items they brought with them. We have a new approach after carrying around far too many papers and random toys, which add weight and limit space for clothing.

We allowed the following for each child;

- A small, A5 or A6 ring-bound notebook (for journalling about the trip, but also for drawing, tearing paper, etc.)
- A pen or a small pack of pencils
- A mini iPad or iPhone
- One small soft toy (if needed)

EXAMPLE:

On our trip to the USA, our youngest, then four years old, brought his favourite small soft toy with him. By the fourth night of a three-week trip, the toy was lost. Cue sobbing child. It was not a good outcome, so now we remind him of that experience and leave beloved toys at home.

We visited Disneyland and Legoland during our trip to the USA, which meant our children purchased many additional items. Having lost his special toy, the youngest wanted a new soft toy. He chose a large "Nemo" fish. In addition, he bought twelve small "Planes" metal toys. These needed to be nestled amongst his clothes for safekeeping. Small metal objects placed inside his shoes and inside the bag did not allow for easy movement through airport security! Therefore, we have learned to limit the number of toys or entertainment items the children bring.

SANITY SAVER TIP:
Toys and entertainment, like certain toiletries, can be purchased at your destination. Remembering this and budgeting accordingly helps you save space in your luggage. After we explained this to the children, they surprisingly left behind the items they felt were absolutely necessary. When we arrived at our destination, they were so busy having fun and exploring that they soon forgot about their toys and entertainment.

'Just in case' items

It took us some time to leave behind a few of the items that appear on the 'just in case' list. Even after several years of travelling with less, my husband still always slipped in a travel clothesline (a long twisted elastic). Now, however, I've weaned him off it, reminding him we can use a standard clothes hanger or the shower rail to air-dry hand-washed items.

Power adapters suitable for each country are another difficult item.

EXAMPLE:

After purchasing a special, multi-country adapter and discovering late at night on our first night in the USA that it didn't work, we learned two things. Firstly, many hotel receptions will have an adapter you can borrow for the short term, meaning that you can purchase one the next day. We found the shop in the lobby sold them for only US$1.50. A much better deal than the AU$40 multi-charger that didn't work.

'What if' items

Here is what I bring to cover our 'what if' scenarios for our family of four:

- A half-strip of paracetamol (approx 4-6 tablets)
- Four (4) Band-Aids
- Ziploc bag with washing sheets

Make it happen. Your actions:

- Consider your trip length and transport choices.
- Research the entertainment options available both for in-flight entertainment and at your destination. For example, back-of-seat screens, colouring books and pencils on the flight, and streaming services, board games, etc. at your destination.
- Check whether items such as a hairdryer are provided at your accommodation.
- Determine if there is a requirement to complete a journal (for example, school-aged children may need to do this if they are missing class)
- Ask your children about the one item (a toy or form of entertainment) they would want with them for comfort or familiarity.

· Add the item to your child's packing list to ensure it won't be forgotten or shoved in at the last minute.

Now that you've considered the extras you may need to pack to keep your children happy and allay your 'what if' concerns, I'll next share how the clothing choices you make can help you travel with less weight.

12

Clothing Choices Can Make or Break

"Memories are who we are. In the end, that's all the luggage you take with you. Love and Memories are what last."
– Kristin Hannah

When you can't just add more space or stuff to a problem, you have to think outside the box. You adapt—constraint forces clarity.

While planning ahead and determining your intention and activities for the trip *(see Chapter 6)* are probably the most important tips for packing light, selecting the right clothing items is also crucial. This is just as applicable to children as to adults, perhaps even more so.

Let's address the most common approach first.

Remove half

This is very popular advice. If you're packing for a larger carry-on size bag, then yes, the 'remove half' advice works well as a starting point.

I used to do this when we first started travelling with less. After too many trips where I came home with unworn items or had moments during the trip where I wondered why I'd brought a particular item, this was my revised process.

It's a very simple approach. Lay out all the clothes you want to pack from your list (which will change depending on the weather at your destination and the activities you plan to do) and aim to pack only half of each item. For instance, if you've pulled out four jumpers (sweaters), take two. Got five pairs of pants? Bring only two, and consider packing a pair of leggings for lounging and to wear underneath if it's cold. If you coordinate your travel capsule wardrobe by colour, everything will match, no matter how little you bring.

Pack for X days

Another popular approach is to pack for a set number of days, regardless of your trip's duration. Having tried this approach, it works well. Especially when utilised with the rest of the tips I share in this chapter and earlier.

It's best explained with an example. If you're travelling for three weeks, as we have done many times, pack clothes for one week. Or, if you're travelling for one week, pack clothes for three or four days.

When weight limits are tight

While the 'remove half' approach is a solid start, and can work well, and packing for a set number of days is also great, neither approach will give you the best outcome if you want or need to pack in seven (7) kilograms or less.

Instead, if, like us, you are flying with an airline that has strict cabin bag limitations and they are vigilantly enforced, or you will be hopping on and off transport as part of your adventure, you may need a different approach.

Or, if you have previously overpacked or felt like you have too much luggage, which is why you are reading this book, then the following approach may be the shift you need to start packing and travelling with less.

> *"We cannot solve our problems with the same thinking we used when we created them."*
> — *Albert Einstein*

The importance of your travel outfit

Your travel outfit refers to the items you wear on the plane or during your mode of transport, and it is a core part of your travel capsule wardrobe. And no, a good travel outfit isn't made up of random things you throw on after you've already packed everything else.

Instead, when you are planning your wardrobe, incorporate a travel outfit. Then plan to wear your heavier items as your travel outfit. In particular, your heaviest shoes and trousers, often jeans, are perfect items to include in your travel outfit, as they are heavy and take up space in your bag.

If you prefer to travel in leggings or similar soft pants, ensure that they are part of your travel capsule wardrobe. For example, if you regularly wear leggings, ensure you have tops that coordinate and that you'd be happy to wear while undertaking the activities you have planned for your trip. Alternatively, if that's not your style, the leggings may be suitable for exercise, sleeping, or as a layer under your other trousers on cooler days.

This applies to children as well.

EXAMPLE:

On our trip to the US, our boys wore what we called travel pants. They were lined with a soft, knit T-shirt-weight fabric, and on the outside, they were made of sturdy cotton. They felt as comfortable as tracksuit pants but looked smarter. Because they were lined, they were warm in the cold climate we were travelling to. In addition, they wore a short-sleeve T-shirt, a long-sleeved cotton button-up shirt, and a lightweight merino wool jumper (sweater). In their bags was a packable down jacket, which became part of the travel outfit for the internal USA domestic flights and train trips where it was cold at both the departure location and destination.

How to pack light, incorporating your travel outfit

Instead of laying out all your clothes and removing half, start with ONE outfit. Again, this applies to both adults and children. For ease, I'll refer to 'you', but please be assured that I also mean 'and do the same for your kids'.

So, back to your ONE outfit. I recommend starting with your travel outfit, as you'll be wearing your heavier clothes and shoes on travel days to keep your bag light and easy to carry. Once you've intentionally selected your travel outfit, add to it as required to provide the maximum number of combinations.

Think in layers and capsules, and then use those to choose outfits.

This approach is probably the opposite of how you might have packed before: you planned outfits first, then packed them. Changing your approach and thinking creatively, which may involve combining items you haven't used together before, can result in needing fewer items overall.

Using the example above and our trip to the USA, we added an extra pair of trousers for each child, long-sleeve Heattech thermals (which could also be worn alone), and a very warm but lightweight fleece top, all of which could be layered when needed to withstand the sub-zero temperatures we'd experience. Plus, underwear and socks. (*For our complete packing list, see the Appendix.*)

You may find, as we have, that adding four, five, or six pieces to your travel capsule wardrobe provides more than enough combinations to cover the entirety of your trip, including the varying weather you will experience.

With that in mind, here are three key considerations when selecting the clothing to pack for yourself and your children.

1. Start with the basics.
2. Lighter-weight layers are always better.
3. Adaptable/flexible options are preferred.

Here is a little more about each of these three.

Start with the basics

Begin with a basic, minimal wardrobe for your planned trip, aiming for a middle ground based on the weather in your destination(s).

Ascertain the time you will spend in each location (and the season there), and your planned activities.

Start with your travel outfit and add a small selection of clothes; then look at suitable swaps or extras to make your basic wardrobe versatile across different seasons (if applicable). Once you have your basics covered, you can adapt and modify as needed to accommodate seasonal requirements.

Assessing the seasons and building in versatility is especially important if you are travelling to multiple destinations with weather variability, as we have done. The variable weather and number of days in each location will then dictate your choices and influence how heavily you lean into one season over another.

EXAMPLE:

When we travelled to Europe in the spring season, the weather was cool and possibly damp. We had three days (out of three weeks) in Singapore, where it was very hot and humid. Therefore, we leaned more towards selecting items appropriate for the majority of our trip, rather than just those three days. However, we kept our days in Singapore in mind when selecting our clothing items and chose to swap some items that might have been useful in cold weather but not in warm weather, for more flexible options (see below). So, rather than including a warm, flannel (brushed cotton) style shirt, each of the boys had a standard cotton shirt, which was suitable for wear in both climates.

Lighter layers are always better

While warm and cosy, heavy woollen jumpers (or sweaters) might seem like an excellent choice for a cold-climate destination, they take up a lot of space and weigh a lot, too. Likewise, the large cotton hooded sweatshirts that my teenagers love to wear at home are not ideal for travelling.

Clever layering is the key to packing light. Selecting items that can be layered together will ensure your limited wardrobe works in both cool and hot weather, providing maximum flexibility with the fewest possible items. This works for both children and adults.

The right type of layers is also important here. Thinner layers are preferable because too many thick layers can hinder movement. Additionally, thinner layers dry faster. With children, you may find you need to spot-wash items where they have been a little messy. Thus, having thinner, quicker-drying items is a huge time-saver.

EXAMPLE:

A short-sleeve T-shirt underneath a long-sleeved button-up cotton

CLOTHING CHOICES CAN MAKE OR BREAK

shirt, and a lightweight yet warm Merino wool jumper, are perfect for the aeroplane.

The short-sleeve T-shirt is suitable for warm climates, as is the long-sleeve cotton shirt with the sleeves rolled up (a bonus is that it covers the arms when sun protection is required). Wearing all these items provides warmth in cooler weather while ensuring maximum flexibility across a range of temperatures. Additionally, wearing layers on the plane means you can carry fewer items in your bag. Win.

Adaptable/flexible options are preferred

As outlined above, layers are your best friend when packing light. To get the most out of your layers, choose clothing that is adaptable or flexible whenever possible. This approach works hand in hand with packing layers.

Which means, when you are selecting your clothing, aim to choose pieces that work together, including layers, even if they are not necessarily your absolute favourite items from your wardrobe.

Why? Because flexibility and adaptability are preferable to having a single favourite.

EXAMPLE 1:

My husband prefers to travel with a very thin, lightweight rain shell instead of a thick raincoat or rainjacket. This one small item provides rain and wind protection and can be worn over a T-shirt or over multiple layers when the temperature drops. He has a 'water-resistant' jacket without a hood, and that works for him too when the rain is light.

EXAMPLE 2:

While I love my down jacket and wear it daily at home during the winter, depending on our destination and the likely duration for each weather type, I will take a packable rain jacket and wear it over a series of thinner layers, rather than carrying a larger, heavier down jacket.

Travel-specific clothing

Plenty of people have asked me about multipurpose or travel-specific clothing. Generally, we are not fond of this type of clothing, especially for growing children. Our theory is that if you don't wear it at home, don't wear it when travelling. Which also means we travel in clothes we are already familiar with wearing. We already know they are comfortable, how well they wear (i.e., how many days we can wear them before they need to be washed), and how we feel good in them. That said, one of our boys loves his zip-off trousers. But he wears them all the time, not just for travelling, so this approach still holds.

Another benefit of this approach is its cost-effectiveness. Travel-specific clothing can be costly, and children grow fast. Between one trip and the next, it's not uncommon for them to need an entirely new wardrobe, especially after a growth spurt. We have clothes, not travel clothes, AND other clothes. Just clothes.

We all like to look presentable when we are travelling. That means being able to move with ease and grace from a day walking in the rainforest or an art gallery to a nice restaurant for dinner. Looking presentable and feeling good makes travelling a lot more enjoyable.

And the kids appreciate this, too. We have found that most children prefer to feel and look good in their clothes. While for many, comfort is paramount (including being warm and, of course, cool enough, depending on the climate), most children we have spoken to want to feel they fit in through their clothing choices.

Which means clothing choices become far more critical in our packing process.

```
SANITY SAVER TIP:
Instead of selecting individual outfits for each day you are
away, choose items that fit into a colour scheme. From those
easy-to-match pieces, you can put together a travel capsule
wardrobe with essentials like a few layering tops, jeans or
trousers, and a jumper (sweater) that can be worn in
multiple ways.
This approach applies to men, women, and children alike! For
women, a lightweight scarf or two can be more versatile and
practical than packing an extra layer. It's easier to change
your look and will be visible in photos, especially since,
as we've found, most photos show you wearing the same coat
anyway.
```

How we do it — the practical steps

Here is exactly how we plan our travel capsule wardrobes.

- Assess the length and duration of the holiday.
- Research weather conditions from previous years for each location/city we are visiting during the travel period.
- Create an initial list for each person based on one easy-to-wear travel outfit, plus additional items we already have in our wardrobes that fit well and offer maximum versatility for clothing and coordination. (Note, I don't do this for my husband, as I figure he's old enough to look after himself!)
- When reviewing the list, I also consider the types of activities we will be undertaking. For instance, if we'll be spending most of our time in cities and visiting museums, we won't need outdoor hiking clothes. If, however, we are mostly hiking outdoors, we need to choose our clothing accordingly. While you might think this is common sense, I have been burned by this mistake before, when we packed the

wrong types of clothes for the activities we were undertaking. It significantly impacted our holiday enjoyment, as we were limited in what we could do because we didn't have the correct attire.

- Review and check the list for colour coordination and specific items in our existing wardrobes.
- Try on ALL clothes to check they still fit (especially important for growing children), and try outfits that have not been worn together previously (relevant for both adults and children).
- Adjust and amend if required.
- Review for sizing, colour and number of items.

Once we have each established a decent travel outfit that includes our heaviest shoes and jackets or jeans, and identified the other items we will be bringing, including accessories, toiletries, and extras, it's time to pack. Not for the final trip, but a trial pack. It's a test to check everything fits and slots in easily.

Make it happen. Your actions:

List each item you will need for the trip (including all non-clothing essentials) and be as specific as possible.

Clothes

1. Establish the travel outfit and any additional outfits that can be created from it, as well as any extra clothes or specific items required for your destination. (Yes, you need to do this for yourself and for children, as this way you know what goes with what and how each item can be mixed and matched.)
2. Review accessories, including hats, scarves, gloves, jewellery (as applicable) and glasses (reading and sunglasses)

3. Lay everything out on your (or the child's) bed.
4. Review for colour coordination.
5. If applicable, remove half (see above)

Extras

1. Think carefully about what precisely you need. Rationalise where you can, substitute and make do where possible.
2. Consider using e-readers, small notebooks, or your electronic devices (such as a phone or iPad) to replace paper and other cumbersome, heavy items, such as reading books.

You can read our packing lists as a guide to the quantity and type of items you may wish to include in the Appendix (*see Chapter 16*).

```
SANITY SAVER TIP:
Keep all the items you know you'll need for the flight -
such as your tablet, headphones, wrap, passport, and pen -
in your handbag or personal item, or, if you are travelling
without a personal item, in a separate pouch inside your
carry-on bag, which makes it easy to grab everything before
stowing your larger bag in the overhead compartment. Not
only will you be able to settle into your seat more quickly,
but it will also prevent you from having to get up
repeatedly to retrieve items you may have forgotten.
And of course, take the same approach for your children,
unless you want to spend the flight popping up and down like
a yo-yo!
```

Now that you've decided on your clothes and have an idea of what extras you need or want to take, in the next chapter, I'll share how to pack efficiently, including the use of packing cubes.

13

How to Pack

"When it comes to luggage, I am an underpacker."
— *Pharrell Williams*

Fitting everything you want to take into a small carry-on-size bag can be one of the primary reasons people feel packing light is too hard. I understand — it can be daunting if you are used to packing a large, checked-in suitcase. However, I'm also assuming that if you've read this far, you're already starting to think differently about your packing and are ready to give it a try.

Firstly, determine how much you *actually* need (*see Chapters 10, 11 and 12*). Many items we routinely contemplate packing are not required if you plan ahead (*see Chapter 6*).

Once you have identified all necessary items, culled and determined your final items that will come with you (*see Chapter 12*), it's all about fitting them into that small bag.

You may have your own unique approach to packing clothes. Some people prefer folding, others roll their garments into tight logs, and others use packing cubes.

We combine all three methods for the best results.

- To maximise space, if you are not wearing your bulkier items such as jeans, trousers, jackets or coats, then fold them.
- Next, roll the remaining clothes tightly to fill any remaining spaces in your bag. For added organisation and to compress your items further, place some of the rolled clothes into a packing cube.
- Additionally, it's helpful to pack loose items, such as socks and underwear, into compression packing cubes, especially if you are using a bag without dividers.

For the children, we often put their underwear, socks, and pyjamas into a packing cube, as this can be easily removed and reinserted into the bag without needing to repack the entire contents.

A few notes on packing cubes

Packing cubes help organise clothing and other items, saving space by compressing contents and making it easier to find specific items. They are generally small, rectangular prism-shaped fabric bags with a zip around the top. Unlike space compression bags used for storing off-season clothes, packing cubes do not require power. Instead, their zip and fabric help compress the items. Additionally, packing cubes allow you to compartmentalise belongings, separate clean from dirty laundry, and protect items from moisture and related smells. As a bonus, they slip in and out of your chosen bag easily, reducing the need to repack your entire bag—especially helpful when travelling with children!

We have mixed views about packing cubes. Some of us love them, others don't.

They are most useful when you want to separate items or use a large single-cavity bag (like a duffel or general backpack). In these cases, packing cubes can help corral smaller items like underwear or keep items for later in the trip (like swimming costumes) separate, clean and contained.

Generally, my husband finds it easier to pack without a packing cube.

However, I use one every trip. Even for a short overnight stay, a few hours drive away, my packing cube is used. When the children were younger, using packing cubes was very useful for inclusion in their bags, as it ensured they could keep items organised and, therefore, repack as needed with ease. Now that they are almost adults, they tend not to use packing cubes.

"Packing is easier when you roll your clothes." Oscar, age 9

How we do it

We always start with a trial pack. That is, a practice run!

- We gather all the items we intend to take/pack for each person, including clothes, toiletries, accessories (such as hats and sunglasses), and additional items (devices, journals, and charging cords).
- Only attempt to do one bag at a time.
- For each person, lay them out on a large, flat surface, such as a bed, and group them by type. For example, shirts should be grouped, underwear kept together, and so on.
- We then roll, or Marie Kondo fold (Google this if you are not familiar), as many of the clothes as we can in advance. For example, with a T-shirt, we fold it in half lengthwise, then roll it from the top/collar down the length, creating a large sausage shape.
- All pre-rolled items are kept together.
- Shoes are assessed for size, shape, and cleanliness, and then placed into a cloth shoe bag, with one shoe upside down on top of the other.

Depending on the size and rigidity of the shoes, you may place a pair of socks, a belt, or underwear inside to maximise space.

- With the bag you have chosen wide open, place the shoes at the base or ends of the bag. (Note – this will vary a little depending upon the type of bag you have chosen)
- It's then a matter of placing each 'sausage' (the rolled garments) into the spaces in a tight, well-fitting way. If it makes sense for your trip, group items in the bag or a packing cube in the order they will be needed. For example, pyjamas near the top or in a separate packing cube are easily accessible if you arrive late at your destination. Or, if you are travelling to a destination colder than your departure location, pack a coat, scarf, and warm hat near the top, making them easy to grab without needing to unpack or even unzipping the bag.
- If it doesn't fit easily, repack. Sometimes, arranging things differently can make all the difference.
- Additionally, at this point, some items may be discarded, as we endeavour to ensure we have only the essentials. We also want to make sure there is always a bit of extra space in the bag. After all, the goal is to make it easy for the children to pack their own bags each time you move from one location to another, so a little extra space is a good idea.
- Once it is confirmed that all items fit into the chosen bag, have the children (depending on their age) pack them accordingly. Fair warning, getting the kids to pack their own bags can be time-consuming, but it's a vital step in ensuring your children can manage their luggage, including packing and repacking it themselves, while you are travelling. Initially, you will need to oversee the process and may be required to assist. However, after a few attempts with gentle encouragement and guidance, most kids manage to pack their bags quite well.

- Note that even after completing a trial pack, further adjustments may still be necessary. Additional accessories or last-minute items often get squeezed in. Invariably, something will have been forgotten in a trial pack, which is why packing with some 'wriggle room' in the bag is the goal from the outset.

SANITY SAVER TIP:
As your children get older, encourage them to take responsibility for this process from the beginning. My teens do this themselves; however, I still (sometimes) check to ensure the colour coordination works and double-check their selections.

Packing with very young children

The above primarily deals with packing clothes for children who are no longer in nappies or diapers. I acknowledge that packing and travelling light with very young children has unique challenges.

Here are some specific tips for packing and travelling with very young children.

- All the tips we have shared remain applicable: research, planning, outfit selection, and trip type.
- Conduct additional research to determine the facilities you will have access to during your trip, including those at airports, on transportation, and at your destinations.
- Depending on your destination country, most places will have nappies or diapers you can purchase upon arrival. This is one of the few times when we recommend planning for worst-case scenarios and encourage you to pack 1-2 days of extra nappies/diapers in your

bag.

- Clothes for very small children are very small! You can pack a few more outfits to account for the outfit changes that are necessary when children are very young.
- Be smart — use your carry-on luggage allowance, which includes a personal item. If your young child is travelling on their own ticket (not as a baby in your arms), they have the same luggage allowance as you. That includes a personal item. For a small child, that may be a nappy bag or small backpack with a day's supply of nappies, two outfit changes, and a small toy or two.
- Cots, prams/strollers, and car seats are all bulky and awkward, making it harder to travel light. Increasingly, these items can be requested or hired for a small fee at your destination. Speciality providers (often founded by other travelling parents) also offer a range of child-related travel items for hire at the destination you are visiting.

Packing with older children and teens

For older children and teens, many of the same approaches apply as for adults. From the age of five, our children have been encouraged to pack their own belongings. And from age seven, with minimal repacking required.

We recommend providing your children with a packing list to assist and checking their choices (yes, even for teenagers!) to ensure they haven't forgotten anything. This method promotes independence and responsibility, helping kids become more involved in preparations while still offering guidance.

Additionally, as previously mentioned (*see Chapter 6*), discuss the weather and planned activities with them. Encourage your children to think about what they believe would be best to pack for your trip, which supports critical thinking and decision-making skills.

Ultimately, supporting your child in packing for themselves (with some guidance and oversight) teaches them valuable, lifelong skills for travelling light and efficiently, fostering confidence and self-sufficiency in travel situations. And as a bonus, it means they know what they've packed, so they can get dressed without fuss and repack it quickly — ideal for travel days.

Make it happen. Your actions:

- Pack one bag at a time.
- Gather all items for each person, including clothes, toiletries, accessories, devices, and chargers.
- Lay out items and group similar items together.
- Fold clothes in half lengthwise, roll into a sausage shape, and keep rolled items together.
- Check shoes for size, shape, and cleanliness; pack in a cloth bag with socks, belts, or underwear inside. Place shoes at the bottom of the bag.
- Pack rolled clothes tightly, fitting them into available space.
- Organise items by necessity, placing essentials where they are easily accessible.
- Adjust and tweak.
- Repack as needed to fit items more efficiently.
- Leave extra space for flexibility.
- Have children pack their own bags to improve skills.
- Adjust packing after trial runs, leaving room for last-minute items.

Well done! If you've taken action, you should now have a packed carry-on bag, or at least have a framework in place to do so. Now, let's pull it all together.

IV

Pulling it all together

"Never have anyone else carry your luggage. Pack only what you need."
— *Karen Finerman*

14

Life Lessons from Travelling Light

*"The more you have, the more occupied you'll be. The less you
have, the more free you are."*
— *Mother Teresa*

In this chapter, I wanted to share eight (8) life lessons we have gained
after travelling with less for more than a decade, to help inspire and
motivate you.

I share the travel insight and how we've taken that learning and
applied it in our everyday lives, too.

Simplify your wardrobe

Travelling with a minimal wardrobe, especially when relying solely on
carry-on luggage, significantly simplifies the morning routine. With
fewer clothing options, the decision-making process becomes almost
instinctive. You naturally select the pieces that you love and that are
appropriate for the day's activities, eliminating the usual time spent
pondering over what to wear. This streamlined approach lets you start

your day more quickly and efficiently, making it easier to stick to your travel schedule.

Application for Life

Streamline your wardrobe at home, too. When we travel light, we only take the clothing items appropriate for the season and planned activities. We can apply this in our everyday lives as well. From boxing up out-of-season items to being clear (and at times ruthless!) about what our current lifestyle requires, we can streamline our wardrobe choices to just those we love and would happily wear every day.

The huge benefit is that you will no longer experience decision fatigue in the morning, and you will feel confident and great in your chosen outfit—just like you do when you're travelling.

Embrace a morning routine

When we are travelling, our morning routine is reasonably predictable. Without the distractions of home, we spend time connecting over breakfast and planning our day. After all, the priority is getting out and enjoying the day in the holiday location.

To this end, we have focused on the essentials—what is essential in the morning to ensure we all have a great day?

My regular morning routine is streamlined to a short meditation, a few quick yoga stretches, a cup of my favourite herbal tea, and a healthy breakfast. For my husband, his non-negotiables include an early morning run, breakfast, and coffee.

Application for life

Instead of a complicated morning routine, a simple one helps keep things clear, calm, and consistent. We can apply the same approach in our everyday lives. Determine your non-negotiables for the morning.

Like me, it might include some yoga stretches or time to meditate. Or, like my husband, you may not feel ready for the day without your caffeine fix.

Enjoy a clutter-free environment

Generally, when we travel, we are either in a hotel or at a rental (apartment or the like). What is uniformly the same across all accommodation types is that they are uncluttered, free of the everyday detritus and debris that visually distract and slow us down.

One of the main reasons we love to travel is to escape the everyday. Think how calming it is when you enter a hotel room – they have the bare minimum of what's required and none of the extraneous items that we generally have at home.

There are no piles of paperwork on the credenza or bedside table; there are no random items left around that you still need to deal with or pick up.

Similarly, when we are travelling light, we aim to minimise the extras we bring. Whether choosing a Kindle or an iPad for reading rather than a pile of books, or keeping all information on a single device rather than multiple bits of paper, the outcome is the same: minimal stuff! Particularly when travelling with carry-on only luggage, it is imperative to leave extraneous items at home.

<u>Application for life</u>

As shared above, the joy of walking into a clutter-free hotel room or rental is well known. However, it may not be achievable to maintain such an environment while living in your home. That said, there are lessons we can take from it and apply to our lives.

Whether it's putting items away, ensuring every item has an allocated spot, choosing to live with less, or being intentional about what we allow into our home in the first place, all of these practices help keep our spaces clutter-free.

The experience of both my clients and myself shows that when we simplify, streamline, and declutter our commitments and belongings, we gain greater mental clarity. This clarity can serve as the impetus to start our next project, set a new goal, or embark on a new chapter in life. And, with that increased clarity comes greater self-confidence. When we know who we are, our values, and where we're going, confidence radiates from us.

Focus on the top three

When we travel, we focus on just the top few items we are most keen to do or see that day, whether it's a must-see attraction, an art gallery we have been looking forward to visiting, or, as the kids would request, a local theme park.

To ensure our holiday remains a holiday and not a marathon, we generally limit ourselves to no more than three activities per day. Three sounds like a lot, but when you're up and out early (as we frequently are with children), three can be quite achievable.

Indeed, we can always do *more* than three things each day. This is where travelling light and embracing simplicity and spaciousness come into their own. Over breakfast or in advance, we will decide on the top three activities or attractions to visit that day or in that city or location.

Sometimes, the attractions are so big that it makes sense to focus on the top three for the duration of our visit. For example, in Los Angeles, our top three were 1) Disneyland, 2) Disneyland, and 3) seeing the Hollywood sign.

We used the same approach each day, too. By prioritising, we determined the top three rides to focus on each day. Once we had incorporated those and planned the best way to avoid extensive queues, everything else was a bonus. So, at Disneyland, any other rides we went on, plus the shows and street performances, were a bonus!

<u>Application for life</u>

Focusing on and prioritising your top three activities or tasks each day is a well-known way to streamline your to-do list and your life. I encourage my clients to take a broader view and consider the top three activities or tasks that align with their values, which will help them move toward their goals or ideal lives.

When we clarify our top three, whether the night before or that morning, we keep things simple, clear, and achievable. And because it's more achievable, we generally do it. Ensuring our actions and tasks align with values and move us towards our goals means we are connected with what matters and less likely to be distracted by busy work or other people's demands.

As in the travelling examples, when we achieve our top three, anything else is a bonus that can be celebrated!

Review and reflect daily

At the end of every day when we're away or travelling, we routinely ask our kids, 'What was the best thing about today?'

While it would be ideal for them to complete a travel journal, it has proven more challenging with my kids. Certainly, I complete the journal at the end of each day, noting activities, what went well, and what we enjoyed most. And I ask the kids similar questions. Generally, over dinner, we will discuss our day, reflect on what worked really well, and share what each of us felt was the highlight of that day.

Through this process, we encourage the kids to reflect, review, and solidify their memories. Additionally, we are practising gratitude. All of these are positive and help remind us that experiences are far more important than possessions, and they are even better when shared with others.

When we travel, we slow down a little, appreciate the moment and enjoy reflecting upon and reminiscing about the experiences we have shared. Whether it's remembering a favourite meal or a funny situation, memories are solidified and elevated through retelling stories and hearing each other's perspectives about the same experience.

Application for life

Many of us go about our day and life in a constant state of perpetual motion. We are always moving forward and rarely pause to look back, reflect, contemplate or celebrate our accomplishments.

Taking time to pause, reflect and determine the best parts of your day, week, or month helps you appreciate your life more. It's easier to acknowledge all you've experienced when you take even just a few minutes to reflect upon what you've learnt, what you've shared and how you have been living in line with what matters most to you.

Generally, in our careers, we are more likely to reflect on our performance due to the standard processes most organisations employ, such as mid-year or annual performance reviews. And these can be incredibly valuable experiences. We generally learn a great deal about ourselves.

However, many of us don't reflect upon our lives in general. Comparing ourselves to others is the exception, not the rule. Without intentional reflection, our experiences blur together, making it difficult to see our progress or recognise the quiet ways we're growing.

And because life moves quickly, we often miss the small moments that could teach us something meaningful if only we paused to notice them.

By taking the time to reflect on and learn from our past experiences, as well as celebrate our accomplishments, we cultivate a habit of appreciation. We also foster a growth mindset. In practice, this looks like giving ourselves permission to be beginners, to make mistakes, and to trust that each step—smooth or messy moves us forward. It shifts our inner dialogue from self-criticism to curiosity, helping us respond to our experiences with more compassion and confidence.

Through this habit of gratitude and an attitude of learning, we live more aligned with our values, focus on what truly matters to us, simplify our lives, and, of course, feel more confident.

When we can see that we are living in alignment with our values, appreciate that we are learning, and prioritise what matters, our confidence naturally increases.

Embrace a slower pace

When we change what we do, time seems to slow down, and that period becomes more memorable. Variety and change actually make us perceive that time is passing more slowly. Travelling for a holiday or vacation is a great example. Time feels like it expands.

Indeed, we perceive that time passes more slowly as we do new things, visit new places, and try new foods on our travels. A three-week break can feel like an incredibly long and full time compared with the three weeks we spend doing our usual activities. Even minor changes to our routine, such as a 'staycation', can have these time-slowing benefits.

When we are vacationing or travelling, we remember specific moments from a holiday, but not the details of our everyday life. I know that I can remember the specifics of where we went, what we did and saw as well as what I wore and ate for a day that was in the middle of a holiday period, but when the day in question is in the middle of a routine week, I have a hard time remembering anything beyond the simple high level detail of being at work or at home!

Application for life

How can we make the day-to-day less routine and more memorable? For most of us, the answer we think of is to take a holiday! Which, of course, is always a lovely idea. However, when a holiday is not possible (because let's be honest, most of the time it's not really feasible for us to go away), what can we do?

We make adjustments to our day-to-day routine.

Examples of things you might like to do to change your routine and feel time slow down:

- Take a course in something new and different
- Have a picnic or eat outside once a week/ every day
- Commit to a new exercise regime, or try a new type of exercise
- Learn a new skill or hobby
- Re-read your favourite author /novels
- Commit to having a weekly dinner date with different friends
- Do something else that you feel is fun!

Timing when we change routine is always essential, and can be a reason to procrastinate. So, here are some ideas for when you might want to slow time and make memories:

- For a season, e.g. winter or summer
- For a month (or two!), when you want to commit to doing something new or different, such as learning a new skill, or want to make that time more memorable.
- School break or holidays

With the feeling that time is passing too quickly, as parents, we often feel that '**the days are long but the years are short.**' The time when our children are happy to do things and hang out with us can slip away when we are caught up in our day-to-day routine. So, when they are on school break, even if you can't travel, it's an ideal opportunity to change routines and make memorable moments together. Both you and your children will enjoy the fun that comes with a change in routine.

The key to all routine change is that doing things a bit differently can bring back an element of fun to your life, make time spent together more memorable, and therefore give you the feeling that time has slowed.

Simplify meals

For us, travel is made all the more enjoyable due to the experience of fabulous food. We love trying new restaurants, new cuisine and experimenting with new tastes. We have also encouraged our children to do the same.

To that end, we actively explore different dinner options and frequently have lunch on the go. It can still be something simple like soup and a sandwich for lunch, and a local cuisine for dinner.

However, breakfast is a meal that we generally have in our accommodation when we are travelling. And they are uniformly simple. We don't have a wide range of options because we will only be in our location for a short time. Therefore, it doesn't behove us to have multiple food choices that will go to waste when we move to our next location.

Instead, breakfast is a simple affair, and we prioritise the foods we enjoy, providing a nutritionally balanced start to the day. For us, that means a bowl of cereal with milk and some fresh fruit, herbal tea for me and coffee for my husband.

Application for life

Considering where and how you can simplify daily tasks, such as meal preparation, planning, and eating, is one way to simplify your life and gain greater clarity. When choice is limited or nonexistent, there is no need to make a decision, freeing you to use your mind for other things!

My clients frequently cite decision fatigue as a major contributor to their desire for greater simplicity.

When we are travelling, simplifying just one meal of the day can help minimise decision fatigue and streamline our meal planning, preparation, and eating time.

And of course, which meal you choose to simplify is up to you. When travelling, for us, breakfast makes sense. At home, we apply the same approach to lunch.

By simplifying our meal choices, we streamline the process and minimise the decision-making required for everyone, which frees up time and energy to engage in other, more exciting activities.

Prioritise fun

Of course, we generally travel because it's vacation time for us, so prioritising fun is a no-brainer! Specifically, when travelling with children, ensuring there are adequate moments for play and fun is key to a successful holiday. That can include downtime or time spent in a local park, playground or, as my boys would always prefer, a local theme park.

By prioritising fun, we create incredible memories and, at the end of the day, have tired, happy family members. And after all, as parents, this is what most of us hope for from a vacation.

Application for life

As adults, many of us no longer prioritise play and fun. We are so busy working and maintaining a hectic schedule, and dare I say it, 'keeping up with the Joneses', we forget to take time for fun.

Travel offers all of us, children and adults alike, opportunities for enjoyment, exploration, learning, and escapism, like how children experience play and fun. As adults, we often travel for pleasure, adventure, and to engage with new experiences, making travel a form of recreation and a chance to de-stress, discover, and connect with the world and ourselves, much like a child playing.

Travel is play for adults.

Play is essential for well-being, as playful activities like travelling to a new place, trying a new food, or experiencing something new boost our energy. Additionally, taking time out to travel, explore, and have fun can restore our sense of balance and equilibrium, helping us reconnect with our passions, sense of self, and soul.

Of course, relaxation is another benefit of travelling light. It can be very relaxing to remove ourselves from the everyday pressures and simply be!

As parents, play is beneficial for our kids, too! And not just for them; it is good for them to see **US** being playful and to experience time with us when we are light-hearted, which is hopefully how we feel when we are on holiday with our children. This playfulness helps foster stronger, more positive relationships and create wonderful memories together.

When we contemplate all the things that are fun and that encourage our curiosity and sense of wonder at the world, we feel lighter. Perhaps we walk with a little more bounce in our step or feel a smile tugging at our mouths. The anticipation of something playful and fun can spark our sense of joy and excitement.

I hope that these insights inspire and motivate you to consider the ongoing benefits you will gain by choosing to travel with less. It truly can be life-changing.

15

TL;DR* — The Summary

*"I enjoy the preparatory elements of travel – packing my bags
and choosing my outfits – but my favourite part is getting there."*
– Dominic Monaghan

I heard you. When I shared with friends and family that I was writing
this short book, several people said, 'I just want the basics! I don't have
time to read the whole book, so tell me what I need to know.'

For those who prefer to skip to the end or read in list format, here is a
high-level summary of what you need to know.

5 P's – the essence of travelling light

When thinking about travelling light, specifically the packing, let's break
it down into the 5 P's.

Plan

- Plan ahead for what you think you'll need. Base this on the research you've undertaken about the weather, the types of activities you'll be doing, and the type of clothes you and your children are most comfortable in.

Prepare

- Prepare for the fact that to travel light successfully, you will need to do laundry. Yes, there it is. This is one of the most significant and vital mindset shifts to make. Once you get your head around the fact that you will need to wash some clothing while you are travelling, travelling light becomes much easier.

Predict

- Think about and predict the types of problems or issues you may encounter during the trip. For example, is your child still very young and requires frequent changes of clothes? If so, you may wish to allow extra clothing for that child. Or, as we have experienced, do you have a child with a knack for spilling their food (on themselves and others)? If so, you may want to select clothing made from quick-dry fabric or coloured fabrics that won't show dirt/spills as much.

SANITY SAVER TIP:
Baby wipes and hand wipes are great for quick spot cleaning and require no water, making them carry-on friendly.

Prioritise

- Lay all the clothing and extra items out for each person. Review, cull, and edit. This is key! Do you need three different jumpers (sweaters) when you'll be wearing the same coat or jacket in every photo anyway? Do the kids really need eight pairs of underpants? Perhaps five would be enough, and you'll hand-wash them every few days.
- Prioritising what you really need and, similarly, what your children really need is essential, as it's the best way to simplify and ensure you carry only what you actually need.

Practice

- Yes, really! Practice packing your bag with the items you have selected. This includes all the extra items—the non-clothes items. Pack the toiletries, the charging cables, the paperwork, the hand wipes, the devices—everything!
- Get your kids to practice packing their own bags, too, so you know they can do it and that when *they* pack their bags, all items still fit. (You really don't want to have to be in charge of everyone's packing—that is too much for each morning when you are on the move.)
- Check there is still some space left, as you will want a little room for souvenirs. Plus, dirty clothes always take up more space than clean ones!

*TL;DR (Too Long, Didn't Read)

There you have it — a 500-odd-word summary of the book. If you have read each chapter, noted the tips, and taken the suggested actions, you and your children should be ready now to travel with less.

Now it's over to you. Start small, try one trip, and give yourself the chance to experience the freedom that comes with carrying less. Your next journey is the perfect opportunity to pack with intention and discover how much calmer and more capable you feel when you're not weighed down by "just in case" items. Trust that lighter luggage leads to lighter days—for you and your children—and you may find you never want to travel any other way.

16

Appendix

Our Packing Lists

I have included a few of our packing lists here as examples so you can get a sense of how many items can fit in a carry-on-size bag for adults and children alike.

Northern Hemisphere Winter

- cold climate
- domestic size carry-on
- carry-on restrictions based on **dimensions**, not weight

Adult – Female

Heattech (Uniqlo) crew neck – White (2), Black (1)

Heattech (Uniqlo) roll neck – Black (1)

Merino t-shirt (thermal – but can be worn by itself) - blue

Jeans – skinny – Black (1)

Jeans – skinny – Blue/regular (1)

Merino cardigan – Black (1)

Merino roll neck – Black (1)

Blue stretchy (wool) dress (1)

Blue pashmina wrap (1)

Patterned large scarf (1)

Small scarf (1)

Down jacket (1)

Black Thinsulate beanie (1)

Black leather gloves (1)

Merino leggings (1)

Thermal leggings (1)

Merino long-sleeve thermal (1)

Tights (black) (1)

Underpants (5 pairs)

Bra's (2) – one black, one beige

Camisole (1) – beige

Icebreaker wool socks (5 pairs)

Long sleeve cotton T-shirt (1) – white (for hotel/sleeping in)

Sleep/leisure pants (1) – black & white (for hotel/sleeping in)

Caterpillar Boots (Patent leather, blue)

Ecco lightweight sneakers (black)

Knitted socks (1) – (for hotel/sleeping in)

+ toiletries, jewellery, iPad, iPhone, journal, pens, electronic chargers, wet wipes, tissues, hand sanitiser, etc.

Adult Male

Merino trousers

Cotton navy trousers

Merino black Short-sleeve thermal (times two)

Merino thermal leggings black (times two)

Icebreaker Merino socks (5 pairs)

Long-sleeve running shirt
Running shorts
Running shoes
Gortex hiking shoes
Merino black hooded jumper/sweater
Flannel shirt (2)
Long sleeve cotton shirt – lightweight
Thinsulate beanie
Gortex gloves
Underpants (5 pairs)
Packable small rain jacket
Cotton T-shirt and boxer shorts (for sleeping in)

Child 1 (age 8)
Travel pants* - black
Jeans – blue
Heattech roll neck – black (1)
Flannel shirt - orange, black & white (1)
Long sleeve cotton t-shirts (3) – one for hotel/sleeping in
Fleece top – blue (1)
Merino cardigan – blue, grey, black & white stripes
Thermal leggings (2)
Thermal top (1)
Down jacket
Beanie & gloves (thermal)
Scarf (knitted)
Soft cotton pyjama pants (for sleeping in)
Cotton Singlets (2)
Underpants (5 pairs)
Socks – wool/ski (3 pairs), regular (2 pairs)
Black leather Converse

White leather sneakers

Knitted socks – for hotel/sleeping

Child 2 (age 4)

Travel pants* - black

Jeans – blue

Heattech roll neck – black (1)

Flannel shirt - green, black & white (1)

Long-sleeve cotton t-shirts (2)

Jumper/sweater – black & grey (1)

Merino cardigan – grey

Thermal leggings (2)

Thermal top (1)

Down jacket

Beanie & gloves (merino)

Scarf (knitted)

Soft cotton pyjamas (for sleeping in)

Cotton Singlets (2)

Underpants (5 pairs)

Socks – wool/ski (3 pairs), regular (2 pairs)

Black leather sneakers

White leather sneakers

Knitted socks – for hotel/sleeping

*Travel pants were the name we gave to the lined trousers we purchased for the children. They were regular, slim-fit trousers with a cargo pocket in black, but were lined with very soft, t-shirt-style fabric. This provided extra warmth and increased the trousers' resilience, allowing them to be worn for multiple days without washing.

Northern Hemisphere + Asia (spring/hot & humid)

- mixed weather trip
- mild to cold climate plus hot and humid
- domestic size carry-on
- carry-on restrictions were based on **weight** (less than seven (7) kilograms per person + one personal item)

Adult – Female

Heattech (Uniqlo) crew neck – White (2), Black (2)

Merino t-shirt (thermal – but can be worn by itself) - blue

Jeans – skinny – Blue/regular (1)

Merino cardigan – Black (1)

Merino (wool) dress – turquoise (1)

Merino scarf - turquoise (1)

Cotton patterned scarf - turquoise (1)

Down jacket (1)

Tights (black) (1)

Underpants (5 pairs)

Bra's (2) – one black, one beige

Camisole (1) – beige

Icebreaker wool socks (5 pairs)

Long sleeve cotton T-shirt (1) – white (for hotel/sleeping in)

Sleep/leisure pants (1) – black & white (for hotel/sleeping in)

Long (under knee) leather boots – black

Flat leather sandals - silver

Knitted socks (1) – (for hotel/sleeping in)

Swimming costume (1)

+ toiletries, jewellery, iPad, iPhone, journal, pens, reading book, electronic chargers, wet wipes, tissues. Etc.

Adult Male
  Navy Cotton trousers (1)
  Running shorts (1)
  Running shirt (1)
  Running shoes
  Gortex waterproof shoes
  Jacket
  Shorts (cotton)
  Long-sleeve cotton button-down shirt (2)
  Merino black thermal T-shirt (1)
  Merino Sweater/jumper
  Cap
  Purchased in Singapore – thongs.

Child 1 (age 9)
  Jeans (2) – blue, black
  Cotton shorts – beige/cream
  Heattech roll neck – navy (1)
  Cotton T-shirt – navy (1)
  Flannel shirt – turquoise, navy & orange
  Long-sleeve cotton, button-down shirt (2)
  Merino jumper/sweater – turquoise
  Down jacket
  Soft cotton pyjama pants (for sleeping in)
  Underpants (5 pairs)
  Socks – wool (2), regular (2)
  Black leather Converse
  White leather sneakers
  Knitted socks – for hotel/sleeping
  Swimming costume
  Baseball cap

Child 2 (age 5)

Jeans – blue

Pull on trousers - navy

Cotton shorts

Heattech roll neck – black (1)

Long sleeve, button-down cotton shirt (1)

Long sleeve, button-down linen shirt (1)

Cotton short-sleeve T-shirt - navy

Merino cardigan – striped

Thermal top (1)

Down jacket

Soft cotton pyjamas (for sleeping in)

Underpants (5 pairs)

Socks – wool/ski (3), regular (1)

Black leather sneakers

White leather sneakers

Knitted socks – for hotel/sleeping

Swimming costume

Baseball cap

Adult Female Make-up / Toiletries (those marked with * were liquids and carried in a Ziploc bag)

BB cream *

Eyebrow pencil

Eyeliner

Lip liner

Pressed powder compact

Lip-gloss *

Lipstick *

Deodorant *

Razor

Toothpaste *
Toothbrush
Face wipes
Night cream *

Child Toiletries (those marked with * were liquids and carried in a Ziploc bag)
Deodorant *
Toothpaste *
Toothbrush
Face wipes
Shampoo*
Body wash*

Sun cream was purchased in Singapore.

About the Author

Rowena Mabbott is a Certified Life Coach and writer who loves travelling with less. She and her family have been travelling internationally and domestically with carry-on only luggage since 2014. This is her first non-fiction book. She also writes contemporary fiction and monthly articles for her coaching business. When she is not wrangling her teen boys or walking the family dog, Rowena enjoys planning their next travel adventure, reading, singing, and spending time with her husband.

You can connect with me on:
🌐 https://www.rowenamabbott.com

Subscribe to my newsletter:
✉ https://www.rowenamabbott.com/love

Also by Rowena Mabbott

Rowena's fiction books explore the complexities of relationships; romantic, familial and platonic.

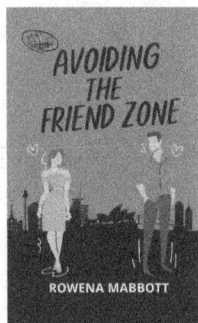

Avoiding The Friend Zone - Single in Sydney Book 1

Two ambitious graduates, Jon and Kate, navigate their careers and an emerging romance in the bustling city of Sydney in a story that will have you cheering them until the very end.

*Avoiding The Friend Zone is a sweet workplace love story with a HEA (happily ever after). It's the first book in the interconnected **Single in Sydney** series, but can also be read as a stand-alone story.*

Available as an ebook and in paperback.

https://books2read.com/b/avoiding-the-friend-zone

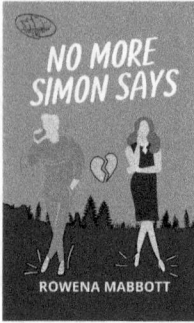

No More Simon Says - Single in Sydney Book 2
Penny believes Simon is the one until he breaks up with her after his father's infidelity is revealed. Heartbroken, she leans on her friends and begins moving on, even developing feelings for a colleague. Meanwhile, after a near-death experience, Simon wants her back, but Penny must decide if rekindling their romance is what she truly wants.

*No More Simon Says is a sweet 'second chance at love' story with a HEA (happily ever after). It's the second book in the interconnected **Single in Sydney** series and can be read as a stand-alone story.*

Available as an ebook and in paperback.

https://books2read.com/b/no-more-simon-says

www.ingramcontent.com/pod-product-compliance
Lightning Source LLC
LaVergne TN
LVHW050045090426
835510LV00043B/3027